Canadian
Daily Language Activities

—— Grade 4 ——

Written by Eleanor M. Summers

Our Canadian Daily Language Activities series provides short and quick opportunities for students to review and reinforce skills in punctuation, grammar, spelling, language and reading comprehension. The Bonus Activities that follow each week of skills are fun tasks such as word and vocabulary puzzles, figurative language and reading exercises. A short interesting fact about Canada is the finishing touch!

ELEANOR M. SUMMERS is a retired teacher who is still actively involved in education. She has created many resources in language, science and history. As a writer, she enjoys creating practical and thought-provoking resources for teachers and parents.

Published in Canada by:
On The Mark Press
15 Dairy Avenue, Napanee, Ontario, K7R 1M4
www.onthemarkpress.com

Funded by the
Government
of Canada

SSR1147   ISBN: 9781771587334 © On The Mark Press

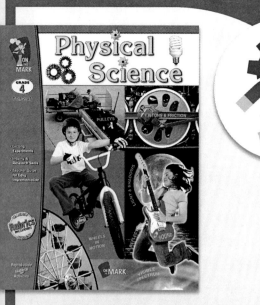

Topics cover:

Pulleys and Gears; Wheels and Levers; Building Devices and Vehicles that Move; Light & Sound; and Shadows.

#OTM2147

Topics cover:

Rocks, Minerals, & Erosion; Weather; and Waste & Our World.

#OTM2155

#J184

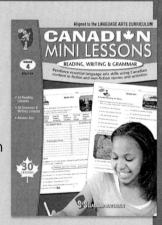

The stories, concepts, and skills are grade appropriate and aligned to the Canadian Language Arts curriculum. This resource consists of two parts:

Reading Skills
Offers reading experiences in a variety of genres and extends the stories with real life applications.

Grammar & Writing
Activities to practice and reinforce vocabulary development, spelling, grammar, punctuation and creative writing.

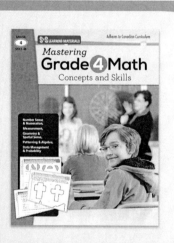

This Mastering Math book is 100% Canadian content following the elementary mathematics curriculum guidelines. Organized according to these five general curriculum threads: Number Sense & Numeration, Measurement, Geometry & Spatial Sense, Patterning & Algebra, and Data Management & Probability.

#K146

HOW TO USE CANADIAN DAILY LANGUAGE ACTIVITIES

This book is divided into 32 weekly sections.

Each weekly section provides daily skill review and assessment activities.

ACTIVITIES 1 – 4

Focus is on:

- punctuation, capitalization, grammar, and spelling
- language and reading comprehension skills

ACTIVITY 5

Focus is on:

- a single language or reading skill

BONUS ACTIVITY

Provides opportunities for extended activities.

- word puzzles, vocabulary development
- spelling
- reading skills
- includes a short, interesting fact about Canada

STUDENT PROGRESS CHART

- Students record their daily score for each Language Activity.
- At the end of the week, they calculate their Total Score
- At the end of four weeks, students evaluate their performance.
- Students will require one copy of page 3 and three copies of page 4 to record results for entire 32 weeks. Teachers may wish to make back-to-back copies.

TEACHER SUGGESTIONS

- All activities may be completed for each week or teachers may exclude some.
- New skills may be completed as a whole class activity.
- Bonus Activities may be used at teachers' discretion.
- Correcting student work together will help model the correct responses.
- Monitor student mastery of skills from information on the Student Progress Chart.

SSR1147   ISBN: 9781771587334 © On The Mark Press

_____'S PROGRESS CHART

How many did you get correct each day? Record your score on the chart.

Week	Activity 1	Activity 2	Activity 3	Activity 4	Activity 5	Total Score
#	/5	/5	/5	/5	/5	/25

Week	Activity 1	Activity 2	Activity 3	Activity 4	Activity 5	Total Score
#	/5	/5	/5	/5	/5	/25

Week	Activity 1	Activity 2	Activity 3	Activity 4	Activity 5	Total Score
#	/5	/5	/5	/5	/5	/25

Week	Activity 1	Activity 2	Activity 3	Activity 4	Activity 5	Total Score
#	/5	/5	/5	/5	/5	/25

My strongest skills are _____

My skills that need improvement are _____

The Bonus Activities I liked best are _____

Week	Activity 1	Activity 2	Activity 3	Activity 4	Activity 5	Total Score
#	/5	/5	/5	/5	/5	/25

Week	Activity 1	Activity 2	Activity 3	Activity 4	Activity 5	Total Score
#	/5	/5	/5	/5	/5	/25

Week	Activity 1	Activity 2	Activity 3	Activity 4	Activity 5	Total Score
#	/5	/5	/5	/5	/5	/25

Week	Activity 1	Activity 2	Activity 3	Activity 4	Activity 5	Total Score
#	/5	/5	/5	/5	/5	/25

My strongest skills are _____

My skills that need improvement are _____

The Bonus Activities I liked best are _____

SSR1147   ISBN: 9781771587334 © On The Mark Press

_____ 'S PROGRESS CHART

Week	Activity 1	Activity 2	Activity 3	Activity 4	Activity 5	Total Score
#	/5	/5	/5	/5	/5	/25

Week	Activity 1	Activity 2	Activity 3	Activity 4	Activity 5	Total Score
#	/5	/5	/5	/5	/5	/25

Week	Activity 1	Activity 2	Activity 3	Activity 4	Activity 5	Total Score
#	/5	/5	/5	/5	/5	/25

Week	Activity 1	Activity 2	Activity 3	Activity 4	Activity 5	Total Score
#	/5	/5	/5	/5	/5	/25

My strongest skills are _____

My skills that need improvement are _____

The Bonus Activities I liked best are _____

Week	Activity 1	Activity 2	Activity 3	Activity 4	Activity 5	Total Score
#	/5	/5	/5	/5	/5	/25

Week	Activity 1	Activity 2	Activity 3	Activity 4	Activity 5	Total Score
#	/5	/5	/5	/5	/5	/25

Week	Activity 1	Activity 2	Activity 3	Activity 4	Activity 5	Total Score
#	/5	/5	/5	/5	/5	/25

Week	Activity 1	Activity 2	Activity 3	Activity 4	Activity 5	Total Score
#	/5	/5	/5	/5	/5	/25

My strongest skills are _____

My skills that need improvement are _____

The Bonus Activities I liked best are _____

DAILY LANGUAGE ACTIVITIES SKILL LIST

This book provides many opportunities for practice of the following skills:

VOCABULARY & WORD SKILLS

- word meaning from context
- root words/prefixes/suffixes
- vowel sounds
- spelling
- syllabication
- synonyms/antonyms/homonyms
- contractions

CAPITALIZATION

- beginning of sentences
- proper names/titles of people
- names of places
- titles of books, songs, poems
- names of days, months, holidays
- abbreviations

PUNCTUATION

- punctuation at the end of a sentence
- commas in a series
- commas in dates and addresses
- commas in compound sentences
- commas in simple dialogue
- commas after an introductory phrase
- commas in direct address/parenthetical expressions
- commas after appositives
- periods in abbreviations
- use of colons
- quotation marks in speech
- quotation marks: poems, songs, stories
- apostrophes in contractions
- apostrophes in possessives
- interjections
- punctuation in a friendly letter
- run on sentences
- underlining: books, plays,poems, magazines

GRAMMAR & WORD USAGE

- pronouns
- common/proper nouns
- singular/plural nouns
- possessive nouns
- verb forms
- verb tenses
- double negatives
- adjectives
- correct article/determiner/adjective
- adverbs
- parts of speech
- comparative/superlative
- subject/predicate
- subject – verb agreement
- identifying sentences
- sentence types
- sentence combinations

READING COMPREHENSION

- analogies
- categorization
- cause and effect
- fact or opinion
- fact or fantasy
- fiction or nonfiction
- figurative language
- inference
- simile/metaphor
- idioms, proverbs

REFERENCE SKILLS

- alphabetical order
- dictionary skills
- reference materials
- media sources

SSR1147   ISBN: 9781771587334 © On The Mark Press

Name: _____

Correct these sentences.

1. have you ever been to niagara falls ontario

   _____

2. my friend nicole lives in montreal quebec

   _____

Number these words to show their alphabetical order.

3. _____ buffalo   _____ beaver   _____ bear   _____ bison

4. _____ elm   _____ elk   _____ eagle   _____ eel

Circle the word that does not belong.

5. hockey   lacrosse   football   french fries   soccer

- -

Name: _____

Sentence or not a sentence?

1. Animals in Canada's North. _____

2. There are five Great Lakes in Canada. _____

Correct these sentences.

3. my teacher said that we are going to visit the royal canadian mint in ottawa

   _____

4. don't you agree that canadians are the greatest hockey players

   _____

Common or proper noun?

5. Royal Canadian Mounted Police _____

Name: _____

Use context clues to explain the meaning of the underlined word.

1. We were <u>dumbfounded</u> by the beauty of the Rocky Mountains.

_____

Correct these sentences.

2. our family is going to visit an old viking settlement in newfoundland

_____

3. wouldn't it be fun to pan for gold in dawson city in the yukon

_____

Circle the words that are spelled incorrectly.

4.   elm   mapel   oake   birch   cedar

5.   robin   cardonal   blue jay   eagel   sparrow

Name: _____

Divide each word into syllables.

1. pioneer _____

2. Saskatchewan _____

Correct these sentences.

3. have you ever been to the cn tower asked chloe

_____

4. our teacher read the story called white fang by jack london

_____

Circle the correct abbreviation for "post office"

5.   po.   P.O.   P/O   pst.

SSR1147 ISBN: 9781771587334 © On The Mark Press

Name: _____

Write the word or words that best complete each sentence.

1. Have you ever _____ on an overnight train ride?

   went / gone / go

2. My friend took two days to _____ reading "Underground to Canada"

   finish / done / completed

3. _____ late for school each morning.

   She's / She'd / She'll

4. My uncle's four-wheeler_____ a flat tire.

   gots / have / has

5. Remember that we _____ beside the light pole so we can find it later.

   parks / parking / parked

- -

Name: _____

Bonus Activity

How many words can you make using the letters in the word "CANADA"?

Remember you can not use a letter more than once unless it is in the word more than once. Check your dictionary if you are unsure of the spelling of your answer.

MY CANADA

When in full production, 15 million loonies can be produced per day.

Name: _____

Correct these sentences.

1. they gets lots of snow in northern manitoba

   _____

2. the winners of the stanley cup will have there team photo on telivision

   _____

Write the two words that make up each contraction.

3. doesn't _____   _____

4. she'll _____   _____

Synonym or antonym?

5. windy, blustery _____

- -

Name: _____

Identify each part of a friendly letter.

1. Dear Mandy _____

2. 24 Sussex Drive _____

Fact or fantasy?

3. Wheat only grows in Saskatchewan. _____

Correct these sentences.

4. a train ride through the rocky mountains wood be a grate adventure

   _____

5. what a terrific save my friend charlie made during the soccer turnament

   _____

SSR1147   ISBN: 9781771587334 © On The Mark Press

Name: _____

Write the root word (base word) for:

1. unexplained _____

Correct these sentences.

2. have you herd the story of how the bluenose wun her first race

_____

3. caribou beaver and the polar bear appear on canadian coins

_____

What do the words in each group have in common?

4. Ontario; Manitoba; Newfoundland; Nova Scotia; Quebec _____

5. Oilers; Maple Leafs; Canadiens; Flames; Canucks _____

Name: _____

Correct these sentences.

1. will you be hour master of ceremonies for the school concert asked miss dunn

_____

2. i would love to meat my penpal from nunavut said reese

_____

Use context clues to explain the meaning of the underlined word in this sentence.

3. You had better <u>pretreat</u> that stain on your T-shirt before your mother sees it.

_____

Write a common noun for each proper noun

4. Tim Horton's _____

5. Ski – doo _____

Name: _____

Reference sources: atlas, almanac, dictionary, encyclopedia, thesaurus

What reference source would be best to look for information on the following:

1. the location of the St. Lawrence River _____

2. a synonym for the word "shiny" _____

3. the biggest lake in Canada _____

4. the meaning of the word "glacial" _____

5. the foods eaten by the beaver _____

Name: _____

Bonus Activity: The Word about Birds!

Choose the right word from the box to match each clue.

crow   loon   mallard duck   pigeon   robin   swan   vulture

1. I lay blue eggs. _____

2. When I am a male, I have a green head. _____

3. I might like to build my nest in your barn. _____

4. I live on a lake and make a mournful call. _____

5. I am a very graceful bird. _____

6. I like to eat dead animals. _____

MY CANADA

The average Canadian watches 21 hours of television per week.

SSR1147   ISBN: 9781771587334 © On The Mark Press

Name: _____

Correct these sentences.

1. amandas dog had ate puppies last saturday

_____

2. how many spelling wurds did you get write on your test asked dad

_____

Singular or plural?

3. geese _____

4. foxes _____

Circle the words that have the same sound as the "ough" in "tough".

5. though   thought   enough   through   rough

Name: _____

Sentence or not a sentence?

1. The moose is a huge animal. _____

2. Snow on the roads. _____

Correct these sentences.

3. us laughed when we heard the story about paul bunyan making the thousand islands

_____

4. travelling threw the arctic ocean culd be dangerous

_____

Circle the adjectives in this sentence.

5. Our beautiful flag has a red maple leaf on a white background with red bars on the sides.

What do these words have in common?

1. puffin, loon, osprey, swan _____

2. chocolate; vanilla; butterscotch; strawberry _____

Correct these sentences.

3. vicky asked how was your visit with yur grandmother

_____

4. my grandfather was a fisherman in the waters of the grand banks

_____

Give the past tense of this verb.

5. think _____

Tell if the underlined word is a <u>noun</u>, <u>verb</u>, <u>adjective</u> or <u>adverb</u>.

1. Heavy snow covered the ground during the <u>blizzard</u>. _____

2. Strong winds <u>whipped</u> the snow into huge drifts. _____

Correct these sentences.

3. make sure you come to the players meeting on thursday said the coach

_____

4. i need to buy new cleets if i am going to play soccer this year.

_____

Write a good sentence for this pair of homonyms.

5. tale, tail _____

SSR1147   ISBN: 9781771587334 © On The Mark Press

Name: _____

Explain the meaning of the underlined figures of speech.

1. The family in this story were <u>as poor as church mice</u>.

    _____

2. Danny can <u>run like the wind</u>.

    _____

3. Wow! Your new outfit makes you look <u>like a million bucks</u>!

    _____

4. Nick was so excited he was talking <u>a mile a minute</u>.

    _____

5. <u>Time stood</u> still as we watched the final minutes of the game.

    _____

Name: _____

Bonus Activity: Gender Words

Some English words refer to females and some words refer to males.

Choose the right word from the box to match those in the list.

queen mother aunt daughter sister wife grandmother niece

1. grandfather _____   5. son _____

2. husband _____   6. king _____

3. father _____   7. nephew _____

4. brother _____   8. uncle _____

Since 2010, Canada has held the record for the most gold medals **MY CANADA**
ever won at the Winter Olympics.

SSR1147   ISBN: 9781771587334 © On The Mark Press

Name: _____

Correct these sentences.

1. have you ever went skating on the rideau canal in ottawa ontario

_____

2. you can by hot chocolate doughnuts and beaver tails at the canal rink

_____

Circle the word that is spelled correctly.

3. pracktice   practic   pracktise   practice

Circle the words that have two syllables.

4. hockey   lacrosse   basketball   tobogganing   soccer

5. Ottawa   St. John's   Montreal   Windsor   Fredericton

Name: _____

Circle the adverbs in this sentence.

1. We walked slowly toward the girl who was singing softly.

Write the plural form of each noun.

2. knife   _____

3. man   _____

Correct these sentences.

4. harry is the goodest friend that i has ever had

_____

5. don't you wish we culd go to the quebec winter carnival

_____

  SSR1147   ISBN: 9781771587334 © On The Mark Press

Name: _____

Simile or not a simile?

1. The horse can run like the wind. _____

2. We like having hamburgers for lunch. _____

Correct these sentences.

3. mack and me does not get to walk to scool together

_____

4. ellen and hur family have went camping in algonquin national park

_____

Circle the words that does not belong.

5. nickel   looonie   quarter   peso   toonie

Name: _____

Divide each word into syllables.

1. bison   _____

2. Alberta   _____

Correct these sentences.

3. the puffin are newfoundland and labrador's official bird

_____

4. we seed a tall woden lighthouse at peggy's cove in nova scotia

_____

Circle the correct abbreviation for "Northwest Territories".

5. NtTs   NT   NWT   NWTS

Name: _____

Reference sources: atlas, almanac, dictionary, encyclopedia, thesaurus

What reference source would be best to look for information on the following:

1. where caribou live _____

2. the average daily temperature in February in Toronto _____

3. the location of James Bay _____

4. the meaning of the word "tundra" _____

5. the distance a monarch butterfly travels when it migrates _____

Name: _____

Bonus Activity: Canada's Capitals

Solve the puzzle by filling in the correct names of Canada's capital cities.

Iqaluit   Yellowknife   Whitehorse   Victoria   Edmonton   Regina   Winnipeg
Fredericton   Charlottetown   Quebec City   Toronto   Halifax   St. John's

Saskatchewan													
Newfoundland													
Nova Scotia													
Ontario													
Nunavut													
Manitoba													
Alberta													
British Columbia													
Québec													
Yukon													
New Brunswick													
N.W.T.													
P.E.I.													

SSR1147   ISBN: 9781771587334 © On The Mark Press

Name: _____

Circle the cause and underline the effect.

1. Because there was a big snow falling, skiing was great!

Correct these sentences.

2. my frend joe lives in winnipeg with his parants max and ruby

_____

3. wear would you go to catch a frash lobster four your dinner

_____

Give the possessive pronoun.

4. a salmon belonging to a bear _____

5. the telephone belonging to Mr. Brown _____

Name: _____

Number the words in alphabetical order.

1. ____ ski ____ stroll ____ swim ____ sprint ____ saunter

2. ____ leaf ____ luck ____ light ____ lamp ____ love

Correct these sentences.

3. mom's plane landed right on time at toronto international airport

_____

4. i cant wait to go to my friends house in nova scotia this sommer

_____

Give your opinion of the following topic.

5. swimming in the ocean _____

Name: _____

Write the comparative and superlative adjectives for these words.

1. scary _____ _____

2. funny _____ _____

Fiction or nonfiction?

3. Moose like to walk on the roads in Newfoundland. _____

Correct these sentences.

4. walk threw this forast and smell the pyne trees

_____

5. youve made a great presentation on yur project said mr hartley

_____

- -

Name: _____

Circle the cause and underline the effect.

1. Dad forgot to set his alarm, so he was late for work.

Correct these sentences.

2. molly's birthday party will start at 200 pm

_____

3. say did you know that canada is the secund largest country in the wurld

_____

Complete the analogies

4. sleep is to night as work is to _____

5. bite is to dog as sting is to _____

SSR1147   ISBN: 9781771587334 © On The Mark Press

Name: _____

Combine these sentences into one sentence.

1. Bob and I went fishing. We went fishing in Lake Erie. We had fun.

_____

2. We baked cookies. They were for our school's bake sale. They were chocolate chip cookies.

_____

3. We went to see the Musical Ride. Mounties ride on horses. They keep time to the music.

_____

4. Marilyn Bell was the first person to swim across Lake Ontario. She was only 16 years old.

_____

5. Jason wants to go with me. I am going to the movies. His mother said he couldn't go.

_____

Name: _____

Bonus Activity: Homonyms

Homonyms are words that sound the same but are spelled differently and have different meanings. **Solve the puzzles by using a pair of homonyms.** Check your spelling!

BONUS!
ACTIVITY

Clues	Homonyms	Clues	Homonyms
1. a dog has one / a story		5. a vegetable / Have you ___ there?	
2. one who cleans / we ___ a big castle		6. not female / letters and parcels	
3. payment for a ride / not dark		7. huge / part of a fireplace	
4. animal with horns / begin a letter: ___ Sue		8. a bus drives on it / She ___ a horse.	

MY CANADA

In 1932, Toronto, Ontario's Maple Leaf Gardens became the first arena to host a four-sided game clock.

Name: _____

Correct these sentences.

1. dans father have been transferred to a armed forces base in the arctic.

_____

2. was you asleep when i come home last nite

_____

Give the plural of each noun.

3. lady _____

4. shelf _____

Circle the word that is spelled correctly.

5. knowlege   nowledge   knowledge   knowledg

Name: _____

Circle the words that have the same vowel sound as "ow" in "crow".

1. now   low   slow   cow   grow   row

What is this person probably doing?

2. Dad put on his boots, coat and heavy gloves. He went outside and got a shovel out of the garage. _____

3. Miss Todd placed the sheets face down on my desk. She looked at the clock and said, "You may begin." _____

Correct these sentences.

4. watch out that car is not stopping for the red light

_____

5. we getted grandma her favourite cookbook holiday baking at the bookstor

_____

SSR1147   ISBN: 9781771587334 © On The Mark Press

Name: _____

Use context clues to explain the meaning of the underlined word.

1. To be a <u>herpetologist</u> you must have no fear of reptiles.

_____

Give your opinion about each topic.

2. building a snow fort _____

3. climbing a mountain _____

Correct these sentences.

4. did you know that the telaphone were invented by alexander graham bell

_____

5. sam breaked the lock and now he dont have no way to lock the door on his room

_____

Name: _____

Correct these sentences.

1. bill anna and jasmine are in grade for at sir winston churchill public school

_____

2. ali told her mother that she were going rollar bladeing in the park with us

_____

Give the pronoun that would replace the underlined noun.

3. Tommy's books were in <u>Tommy's</u> locker. _____

4. <u>Mom and Dad</u> went out for dinner. _____

Write one sentence using this pair of homonyms: night, knight

5. _____

Write the word that best completes each sentence.

1 _____ you want to come shopping at the mall with us? | Is / Do / Does |

2. Chelsea gave the bookmark she made to _____ . | she / they / her |

3. The _____ on my sweater are falling off. | buttons' / buttons / button's |

4. Grandma's favourite show _____ on at 2 o'clock. | comed / come / comes |

5. Dad _____ typing on his laptop in his office. | was / be / were |

Bonus Activity: Words from Native Languages

Many Canadian words and place names come from Native languages. Match a word in the box with the clue that describes it.

| Winnipeg   canoe   Miramichi   moccasin   kayak   squash |

1. a light boat moved with paddles _____

2. a yellow vegetable _____

3. a soft shoe made of leather _____

4. from "win – nipi" meaning "muddy water" _____

5. from a Cree word meaning "swiftly flowing water" _____

6. an Inuit canoe _____

The coldest temperature ever recorded in Canada was on February 3, 1947.
It was a chilly -63°C in Snag, Yukon!

MY CANADA

   SSR1147   ISBN: 9781771587334 © On The Mark Press

Name: _____

Correct these sentences.

1. where warm close if you is going tobogganing at big hill park

_____

2. french fries gravy and cheese curds is used to make pouteen a favourite canadian treet

_____

Give the past tense of these verbs

3. find _____

4. give _____

Fact or opinion?

5. Canada and the United States share the world's longest undefended border.

_____

Name: _____

Write the plural form for the following nouns.

1. tooth _____

2. canary _____

Where would the following probably take place?

3. The huge ice-breaker slowly made a path for the smaller ships.

_____

Correct these sentences.

4. my favourite NHL teem the montreal canadiens are playing in the montreal forum tonight.

_____

5. robert munsch has writen more than fourty books for chidren

_____

Name: _____

Write a synonym for

1. unhappy _____

Correct these sentences.

2. mrs long said study all 20 words for yur speling test on fryday

_____

3. do you beleive that winnipeg is one of the coldest cities in canada

_____

What do the words in each group have in common?

4. tuna; cod, haddock, smelt; mackerel _____

5. snowshoes; skates; skis; snowboards; bobsleds _____

Name: _____

Correct these sentences.

1. when adam broken his leg he gots to use crutches to get arownd

_____

2. mrs burns said plaes sit quietly during the assembly in the gim

_____

Simile or metaphor?

3. My little sister slept like a baby after playing outside all day.

_____

Write the possessive form of the noun

4. the horns of the buffalo _____

5. the claws of the bear _____

SSR1147   ISBN: 9781771587334 © On The Mark Press

Name: _____

Read the following paragraph. Decide what type of error is found in the underlined parts: *capitalization, punctuation, spelling,* or *no error*.

Canada's name comes from the Huron word "kanata". We know in the Huron <u>languge</u>, <u>"kanata" means small village</u>. How did a large country like Canada
    1   2

get named after a small <u>village.</u> An explorer named <u>jacques cartier</u> first put the
                           3   4

name on the map. A young Native guide pointed to a small <u>settlement</u> and said
                                                              5

"kanata". Cartier thought he meant that was the name of the entire region.

1. _____   4. _____

2. _____   5. _____

3. _____

Name: _____

Bonus Activity: Anagrams

Change the order of the letters in each underlined word to make the correct word.

1. Make <u>lap</u> into a word meaning "friend" _____

2. Make <u>dab</u> into a word meaning "not good" _____

3. Make <u>cask</u> into a kind of bag. _____

4. Make <u>wed</u> into droplets of water. _____

5. Make <u>sale</u> into an animal. _____

6. Make <u>bran</u> into a farm building. _____

7. Make <u>fade</u> into a word meaning "not able to hear" _____

MY CANADA   *Canada is home to about 630 different species of birds.*

Name: _____

Correct these sentences.

1. saskatchewan has the most rodes in all of canada

_____

2. did you know that ringette and 5-pin bowling were invented by canadians asked dad

_____

Write the two words that make up each contraction.

3. wouldn't   _____   _____

4. they're   _____   _____

What is the root word (base word) for:

5. unintentional   _____

Name: _____

Complete the analogy.

1. wing is to bird as arm is to _____

2. run is to horse as fly is to _____

Circle the word that is spelled correctly.

3. janury   January   Janaury   january

Correct these sentences.

4. we recited the pome the cremation of sam mcgee by robert service

_____

5. our plain made an emergancy landing in gander newfoundland

_____

   SSR1147   ISBN: 9781771587334 © On The Mark Press

Name: _____

Common or proper noun?

1. Dr. Banting   _____

2. blueberry waffles   _____

Correct these sentences.

3. do you know the words to the song god save the queen

_____

4. our libary has many good books about canadian explorers

_____

Is this sentence a statement, interrogative, command or exclamatory?

5. Watch the baby while I answer the phone. _____

- -

Name: _____

Correct these sentences.

1. my mom works as a nurse at the hotel dieu hospital i told my friend amy

_____

2. sometimes canada is called hollywood north

_____

Write the word that best completes the sentence.

3. _____ telephone line was busy when I tried to call.

                         Bettys / Betty's / Bettys'

Number these words in alphabetical order.

4. ____ golf   ____ gong   ____ going   ____ gorilla   ____ goat

5. ____ hardly   ____ hanging   ____ happy   ____ hand   ____ handsome

Name: _____

Explain the meaning of the underlined expressions.

1. Try to <u>keep a stiff upper lip</u>. _____

2. We <u>had a bird's eye view</u> from the plane. _____

    _____

3. It is raining <u>cats and dogs</u>. _____

4. She has <u>a frog in her throat</u>. _____

5. He will <u>hit the roof</u> when he hears the news. _____

    _____

Name: _____

Bonus Activity: Same Category

Choose the right word from the box to add to each category.

tennis   mango   otter   daisy   jacket   corn   autumn

1. wheat, barley, oats _____

2. spring, summer, winter _____

3. raccoon, moose, buffalo _____

4. lily, carnation, pansy _____

5. football, baseball, hockey. _____

6. banana, cherry, plum _____

7. trousers, vest, shirt _____

Y CANADA   *In Alberta, over 200,000 pancakes are served during the Calgary Stampede.*

Name: _____

Simile or metaphor?

1.   The damaged boat sank like a stone.   _____

2.   I'm so tired that I think I'll hit the hay. _____

Correct these sentences.

3.   we sang soldiers and sailors at hour remembrance day service

_____

4.   canada shares for of the great lakes with its nieghbour the united states

_____

Circle the subject and underline the predicate in this sentence.

5.   Jerry filled the can with gas for the lawnmower.

Name: _____

Add a prefix to the words.

1.   paint   _____

2.   aware   _____

Subject pronoun or object pronoun?

3.   They delivered the new furniture to our house. _____

Correct these sentences.

4.   nathan where is the puppy's leash asked barb

_____

5.   our cat bubbles loves to sharpin her claws on the scratching poste.

_____

Name: _____

Write the root word (base word) for:

1. unpredictable _____

Correct these sentences.

2. the sledgehammer ride at canada's wonderland are won of a kinde

_____

3. many childrun played beside the creak and in the mudd

_____

How many syllables does each word have?

4. peanut butter _____

5. polar bear _____

Name: _____

Correct these sentences.

1. we was studying jacques cartier in mr roberts class

_____

2. i asked my brother does you wanna go visit grandma on friday

_____

Use context clues to explain the meaning of the underlined word sentence.

3. You had better take your umbrella. That sky looks <u>ominous</u>.

_____

Subject pronoun or object pronoun?

4. <u>We</u> are going to drive along the Cabot Trail. _____

5. We want to see <u>it</u> for ourselves. _____

SSR1147   ISBN: 9781771587334 © On The Mark Press

Name: _____

Write the word that best completes each sentence.

1. Brad and _____ play on the same baseball team.
   I / me

2. Sandy drove the car _____.
   well / good

3. If our team plays _____ , then we will win the championship.
   well / good

4. Will you pass _____ the cookies, please?
   I / me

5. Everyone had a _____ time at the birthday party.
   well / good

Name: _____

Bonus Activity: Something Fishy!

Choose the word from the box to match each clue.

sardines trout eel
spawn gills nets
salmon bass

1. I am a fish that looks like a snake. _____

2. I am a freshwater fish. _____

3. These are the eggs of fish. _____

4. I am the outer cover of a fish _____

5. We are used when catching fish. _____

6. We are used for breathing. _____

7. We are small fish sold in cans. _____

8. I am a fish that travels upstream to lay eggs. _____

IMAX film systems were invented in 1970 by the IMAX Corporation of Toronto, Ontario.

MY CANADA

Name: _____

Circle the word that is spelled correctly.

1. acter   actor   ackter   acktor

2. thair   thier   their   thare

Correct these sentences.

3. i sitted by myself on the bus and sleeped all the way to sault ste marie

_____

4. i readed for chapters in my book wile i were waiting four you

_____

Complete the analogy.

5. Beef is to cow as pork is to _____

Name: _____

Add a prefix and a suffix to each word.

1. read   _____

2. plan   _____

Fact or opinion?

3. That theatre has the best movies in town. _____

Correct these sentences.

4. i thinked you was absent when we voted four class president

_____

5. john mccrae wrote the well known pome in flanders fields

_____

     SSR1147   ISBN: 9781771587334 © On The Mark Press

Name: _____

Number these words in alphabetical order.

1. _____ famous   _____ fuzzy   _____ friendly   _____ faster

Correct these sentences.

2. my teacher miss grant came to hour house for dinner last sunday

_____

3. ella emily and elizabeth went skiing in quebec last saturday

_____

Write the comparative and superlative forms of these adjectives.

4. noisy   _____   _____

5. sunny   _____   _____

Name: _____

Correct these sentences.

1. dont gave up when you furst cant solve the problem

_____

2. we singed the songs jingle bells and frosty the snowman in december

_____

Write a sentence using this pair of antonyms: ate / eight

3. _____

How many syllables in each word?

4. British Columbia   _____

5. Athabasca   _____

Name: _____

Combine these sentences into one good sentence.

1. I chopped the wood. I carried it into the house. I lit the fire.

   _____

2. Dan went on holidays. He packed his suitcases. He put his things in his car.

   _____

3. She baked it in the oven. She decorated it with sprinkles. Mom made a cake.

   _____

4. I read a book. I went to bed. I put on my pyjamas.

   _____

5. Dad bought some paint for my room. He admired his work. He painted my room.

   _____

- -

Name: _____

Bonus Activity: Collective Nouns

Choose the right word from the box to match each clue.

| pack | bale | flock | list | school | set | herd | pile |

1. a _____ of names   5. a _____ of dishes

2. a _____ of wood   6. a _____ of fish

3. a _____ of cows   7. a _____ of birds

4. a _____ of cards   8. a _____ of hay

MY CANADA

Canada is the third largest producer of diamonds in the world. Sparkle on!

SSR1147   ISBN: 9781771587334 © On The Mark Press

Name: _____

Correct these sentences.

1. dontcha wish we cud go to an nhl hockey game in edmonton

_____

2. even though wed be late for school we decided to wate for nathan

_____

Write the correct pronoun to replace the underlined words.

3. <u>Dan</u> lost his money on the way to the candy store. _____

4. <u>Mrs. Briggs</u> told the class to remember to study for the test. _____

Past, present or future?

5. I saw your cousins at the movies. _____

- -

Name: _____

Circle the word that has been correctly divided into syllables.

1. ca – ri – bou   car – i – bou   cari – bou

2. fo – rt – ress   fort – ress   for – tress

Correct these sentences.

3. i told harry that i was visiting my cousins in fredericton during christmas break

_____

4. my uncle hank loves his ford truck but my aunt drives a dodge

_____

Write the root word (base word) for:

5. impossible   _____

Name: _____

Correct these sentences.

1. our family leaved toronto when my dad got a new job in winnipeg

_____

2. sam steve and me have went to soccer camp for too years

_____

Write a synonym for each word.

3. enormous _____

4. puny _____

What is this person's occupation?

5. She brought me a menu so I could order my lunch.

_____

Name: _____

Fact or fiction?

1. Farley Mowatt, a famous Canadian author, wrote many stories about the North. _____

2. All the polar bears in the world live in Canada's Arctic. _____

Correct these sentences.

3. my class are doing an exchange visit with a shool in montreal

_____

4. icebergs can be saw off the coast of newfoundland in april and may

_____

Simile or metaphor?

5. He said he was so hungry he could eat a horse. _____

SSR1147   ISBN: 9781771587334 © On The Mark Press

Name: _____

Write the word or words that best complete each sentence.

1. When we went fishing we _____ five big fish.
    catched / catching / caught

2. Of all the places I have been, I liked Niagara Falls the _____.
    good / better / best

3. My family have _____ to a cottage every July.
    went / gone / going

4. _____ going to wish that they had come to this party.
    Their / They're / There

5. Victor _____ the team for the most points in this game.
    lead / is lead / leads

Name: _____

Bonus Activity: Join to Make One Word

Make new words by writing a word from the box beside each of the words below.

| body brush fly gown ground hopper lid slide stick top |

1. no_____   6. night_____

2. eye_____   7. butter_____

3. broom_____   8. land_____

4. grass_____   9. roof_____

5. paint_____   10. camp_____

MY CANADA

Canada has 41 national parks and 3 marine conservation areas.

Name: _____

Simile or metaphor?

1. The clouds in the sky were marshmallows floating by. _____

Correct these sentences.

2. mr evans said i would like to thank carla and chris for helping organize fun day

_____

3. our basketball team are gonna try hard to wine the championship

_____

Write the correct pronoun to replace the underlined noun.

4. <u>My mom's</u> van can carry seven people. _____

5. <u>The bus</u> will be here at 1 o'clock sharp. _____

- -

Name: _____

Correct these sentences.

1. does you like chocklit or vanilla ice creem the moast

_____

2. uncle peter owns a bate shop on the shure of lake erie

_____

Write the comparative and the superlative forms of the adjectives.

3. tall   _____   _____

4. strong   _____   _____

Fact or opinion?

5. Hockey is the greatest game in the world. _____

SSR1147   ISBN: 9781771587334 © On The Mark Press

Name: _____

Correct these sentences.

1. gimme all your muney the robber growled

_____

2. help help screemed the little old lady

_____

Subject pronoun or object pronoun?

3. We looked for our mitts and found <u>them</u> in the closet. _____

4. Mother gave <u>her</u> the chocolate cake. _____

Write the comparative and superlative form of this adjective.

5. crispy _____ _____

Name: _____

Correct these sentences.

1. when mario buys his knew camera he will take our pickture

_____

2. the sky turned derk and it beginned to poor rain

_____

Fact or fiction?

3. Canada is the largest country in the world. _____

4. Icebergs can be very dangerous for ships travelling near them. _____

What part of speech is the underlined word?

5. The rock band played very <u>loud</u> music. _____

Name: _____

Decide if the underlined parts have a *capitalization error*, **a** *punctuation error*, **a** *spelling error*, **or** *no mistake*. **Write your answer on the line following the sentence.**

1. We have heard people <u>say You are as blind as a bat</u> _____

2. Bats are not blind but find <u>there</u> way by using sound when flying at night.

    _____

3. These sounds <u>bounse</u> back from the trees or other objects.

    _____

4. <u>bats</u> have good ears and can pick up the returning sounds.

    _____

5. Then <u>they</u> can tell how far away these objects are. _____

Name: _____

Bonus Activity: Animal Fathers and Mothers

Use the right word to tell the names of these animal fathers and mothers.

nanny   bull   lioness   hen   sow   doe   mare   drake   ewe   gander

1. A mother chicken is a _____

2. A father duck is a _____

3. A mother lion is a _____

4. A mother pig is a _____

5. A mother horse is a _____

6. A father goose is a _____

7. A mother sheep is a _____

8. A mother deer is a _____

9. A mother billy goat is a _____

10. A father cow is a _____

MY CANADA

Canadians drink more fruit juice per person than any other country in the world. Yum!!

SSR1147   ISBN: 9781771587334 © On The Mark Press

Write the contraction made from these two words.

1. they are   _____

Correct these sentences.

2. excuse me miss how much does this chair cost asked mrs peterson

_____

3. miss abbott reminded us study for your test tomorrow

_____

Write the pronoun that would replace the underlined noun.

4. <u>The truck</u> has run out of gas.   _____

5. Darlene eats lunch with <u>Sarah</u> everyday at school. _____

Complete the analogies.

1. Bill is to William as Bob is to   _____

2. Beth is to Elizabeth as Susie is to   _____

Correct these sentences.

3. on july 1 1867 canada became a country

_____

4. johnny has broke his bicycle chain so hell ask his dad to fixe it

_____

Write one good sentence using this pair of homophones.

5. tale, tail   _____

Name: _____

Number these words in alphabetical order.

1. escort, eleven, evening, error, erosion ,eagle

_____

Correct these sentences.

2. are she saving seats four her for friends at the movie

_____

3. the boys is helping there grandfather plant his gardan on saterday

_____

Write the words that make up each of these contractions.

4. mustn't   _____   _____

5. they've   _____   _____

Name: _____

Circle the correct abbreviation for "metre"

1. M   Mt   m   mr   met

Correct these sentences.

2. my favourite yello flour is a daffodil said mother

_____

3. dad asked did you here my cellphone rang

_____

Write *past*, *present* or *future* for each sentence.

4. We dove into the deepest end of the pool. _____

5. We are getting a new car on Saturday. _____

      SSR1147   ISBN: 9781771587334 © On The Mark Press

Name: _____

Explain in your own words the meaning of the underlined figures of speech.

1. Watching this movie is <u>as much fun as watching paint dry</u>.

_____

2. I <u>was racking my brain</u> to remember the capitals of the provinces.

_____

3. "Just because you're upset doesn't mean you can <u>bite my head off</u>," I said.

_____

4. My cousins know the words to those pop songs <u>by heart</u>.

_____

5. Sally <u>felt blue</u> when she lost the race.

_____

Name: _____

Bonus Activity: Words! Words! Words! About Our Bodies

Use the correct word from the box to complete each sentence.

1. Our teeth grow in our _____

2. Arms and legs are called _____

3. Sweat comes from the _____ in our skin.

4. The _____ pumps blood around the body.

5. Holes in our noses are called _____

6. The _____ protect our lungs and chest.

7. Bones move at the _____

8. A _____ is a decaying hole in a tooth.

| nostrils |
| gums |
| ribs |
| pores |
| joints |
| cavity |
| heart |
| limbs |

MY CANADA

No porcupines, skunks, or poison ivy are found on the island of Newfoundland.

Name: _____

Correct these sentences.

1.　my sister and me falled asleep wile watching the movie frozen

_____

2.　the sign said it was 300 killomtres to toronto so we knew it wood be a long trip

_____

Circle the correct way to divide this word into syllables.

3.　Ma – ni – toba　　Man – i – to – ba　　Man – it – oba

Circle the correct spelling.

4.　carebou　　cariboo　　caribou　　ceribou　　carbou

5.　mukrate　　muskrate　　maskrat　　miskrat　　muskrat

Name: _____

Correct these sentences.

1.　 do these too loads of laundry and then put your close away in yore room

_____

2.　try to make your work neater jack said mrs blake

_____

Give two words that rhyme with each of these words.

3.　time　_____　　_____

4.　meet　_____　　_____

Circle the words that have the same sound as "ow" in "low".

5.　snow　　how　　blow　　grow　　down

　　　　SSR1147　ISBN: 9781771587334 © On The Mark Press

Name: _____

Write the two words that make up each contraction.

1. you've _____   _____

2. he'll _____   _____

Correct these sentences.

3. me and jill went to by a berthday present for emily

   _____

4. her berthday is on friday novembur 13 and her party is on saturday.

   _____

Tell if these words are *synonyms, antonyms* or *homophones*.

5. pain, pane _____

Name: _____

Correct these sentences.

1. they likes to eat sereal and tost for brekfast each morning

   _____

2. he losed some of his socks so now he wares mismatched pears

   _____

Write the pronoun that would replace the underlined words.

3. <u>Dad</u> has to be at work by 7:30 each morning. _____

4. <u>The members of the band</u> marched to the beat of the drum. _____

Use context clues to determine the meaning of the underlined word.

5. You should be certain of your facts before making such a serious <u>accusation</u>.

   _____

Name: _____

Reference sources: atlas, almanac, dictionary, encyclopedia, thesaurus

What reference source would be best to look for information on the following:

1. the average temperature of Edmonton, Alberta _____

2. a synonym for the word "rough" _____

3. the location of Hudson Bay _____

4. what a polar bear eats _____

5. the meaning of the word "tundra" _____

Name: _____

Bonus Activity: Dictionary Detective

Answer these questions by looking up the underlined word.

1. What is molasses made from? _____

2. What time of year would you hear about a Chinook? _____

3. What is calico made from? _____

4. How many musicians play in a quartet? _____

5. What is the value of a toonie? _____

6. Name three main ingredients found in poutine. _____

7. What grows in the tundra region of Canada? _____

MY CANADA

Canadians eat more macaroni and cheese than any other nation in the world.

SSR1147   ISBN: 9781771587334 © On The Mark Press

Name: _____

Write the comparative and superlative form for each adjective.

1. rough   _____   _____

2. rocky   _____   _____

Circle the correct abbreviation for Saturday

3. St.   Stdy.   Sat   Satur.   Sat.   Sday

Correct these sentences.

4. well that job was easy when you helped me i told my sister

_____

5. we herd a loud noize when the tire blue apart

_____

Name: _____

Write the pronoun that replaces the underlined words.

1. <u>Mom and Dad</u> are going away for the weekend. _____

Correct these sentences.

2. did you see the tv special called atlantic marine life on sunday

_____

3. tourists like to take a cruize on the rideau canal in july and august

_____

Write the plural form of the following nouns.

4. fox   _____

5. bunch   _____

Write *sentence* or *not a sentence*.

1. Up the highest mountain _____

Divide the following words into syllables.

2. gigantic _____

3. soldiers _____

Correct these sentences.

4. im allergic to peanuts tree nuts and walnuts chloe said

_____

5. tim is looking for a summer job at jordans garden centre

_____

Write the plural forms for the following words.

1. woman _____

2. tooth _____

Correct these sentences.

3. im sorry that i cant go with you to the quebec winter carnival emma said

_____

4. address those small envelopes and then male then write away

_____

Write two words that rhyme with the following word.

5. soon _____   _____

SSR1147   ISBN: 9781771587334 © On The Mark Press

Read the following paragraph. Decide what type of error is found in the underlined parts: *capitalization, punctuation, spelling,* or *no error.*

Harrison Hot Springs, at the southern tip of <u>harrison lake in british columbia</u> is
1

a <u>poplar</u> tourist spot. Its beach has the best kind of sand for building sand castles
2

because it really sticks together when <u>its</u> wet and packed down. Every September
3

they hold the <u>world championship of sand sculpture</u> there. When they're done,
4

the beach becomes the largest <u>outdoor art show in western Canada.</u>
5

1. _____   4. _____

2. _____   5. _____

3. _____

Name: _____

WEEK
15

BONUS!
ACTIVITY

Bonus Activity: Nouns! Nouns! Everywhere!

Read the words below. Colour the boxes that have words that are nouns.
Hint: you should find eight words.

canoe	splash	wavy	sea - doo
rough	rushing	sailboat	spying
laughing	kayak	nearby	scow
turning	training	ferry	smiling
steamer	sloop	gruff	broken

What category do these nouns fit into? _____

MY CANADA

A whopping 81% of Canada's total population lives in cities.

SSR1147   ISBN: 9781771587334 © On The Mark Press

Name: _____

Write the adverb used in the following sentence.

1.   He skillfully handled the puck, took his shot and scored! _____

Name the part of speech that is underlined.

2.   We <u>remembered</u> everything on our "To Do" list. _____

3.   My brother is learning to play a <u>flute</u> in the school band. _____

Correct these sentences.

4.   we is going campin in algonquin park with our neighbours the browns

_____

5.   the calgary stampede are a grate tourist attraction said my uncle rex

_____

Name: _____

Fact or opinion?

1.   Anna's party dress was the most beautiful one of all. _____

Write two words that rhyme with each of the following words.

2.   give   _____   _____

3.   stone   _____   _____

Correct these sentences.

4.   you coulds join our club if you is able to keep secrets

_____

5.   dodi said i want to be a pilot when i grew up

_____

   SSR1147   ISBN: 9781771587334 © On The Mark Press

Name: _____

Circle the correct way to divide each word into syllables.

1. agree – ment   a – gree – ment   ag – ree – ment

2. wa – lk – ing   wal – king   walk – ing

Add a suffix to make a new word.

3. point   _____

Correct these sentences.

4. jane received the most valuable player award for the seeson

_____

5. we had hambergers french fries and cookys for dinner on friday

_____

Name: _____

Correct these sentences.

1. we gots to get hour bedrooms cleaned up befor Mom gets home

_____

2. do you ride a bus two school or does your parents drive you their

_____

Tell if these nouns are *common* or *proper*.

3. Steve Nash   _____

4. glacier   _____

Write the plural form of this noun.

5. church   _____

Name: _____

Combine the two sentences into one good sentence.

1. Deserts are hot places. Certain plants cannot grow well.

   _____

2. Very little rain falls. The sun and wind dry it up.

   _____

3. Cactus grows in the desert. And so do small bushes.

   _____

4. You can see sand for miles. Sometimes you see rocks.

   _____

5. The desert is a harsh place. Very few people live there.

   _____

- -

Name: _____

Bonus Activity: Water Word Search

Find and circle the following words in the puzzle.

ocean
river
canal
bay
waterfall
rapids
lake
reservoir
dam

m	e	a	s	o	t	b	n	i	r
i	r	d	y	c	e	w	m	r	e
c	o	s	a	r	a	p	i	d	s
m	c	a	n	a	l	x	y	r	e
r	e	p	c	n	o	d	h	u	r
w	a	t	e	r	f	a	l	l	v
p	n	r	i	b	a	m	s	a	o
b	t	e	a	r	d	s	r	k	i
a	w	y	c	s	r	i	v	e	r

MY CANADA

Canada got its own national flag on February 15, 1965.

   SSR1147   ISBN: 9781771587334 © On The Mark Press

Name: _____

Correct these sentences.

1. me and her left for school at the same time this mourning

_____

2. thats the scarier story ive ever read said polly

_____

Write the root word for these words.

3. unpleasant _____

4. sharpener _____

Circle the words that have the same sound as "y" in "cry".

5. fry   baby   yellow   spy   by

Name: _____

Circle the adjective. Does it tell *which one, what kind,* or *how many?*

1. Mystery books are the ones that are read most often. _____

Correct these sentences.

2. i have a dentist appointment with dr macdonald on tues jan 13

_____

3. chuck's dog ringo does not like his cat miss kitty

_____

Complete the analogies.

4. sailor is to ship as astronaut is to _____

5. Hearts are to Valentine's Day as shamrocks are to _____

Name: _____

Tell if the underlined word is a *noun, verb* or *adjective.*

WEEK

17

ACTIVITY

3

1. <u>Snow</u> is falling and sticking to the bushes. _____

2. Dad <u>shouted</u> loudly to his friend across the street. _____

Write a good sentence for this pair of homophones.

TOTAL

/5

3. sore, soar

_____

Correct these sentences.

4. we gots to fix the flat tire on our knew car

_____

5. you did good on your geography project about spain

_____

Name: _____

Fact or opinion?

WEEK

17

ACTIVITY

4

1. Chocolate ice cream is the best flavour of all. _____

2. Our team jerseys are gold and green. _____

Correct these sentences.

3. the diamond players theatre is going to do a play called sleeping beauty

TOTAL

/5

_____

4. has you ever heard the song called small world asked the teacher

_____

Tell if the underlined part is the *subject* or the *predicate* of the sentence.

5. The train <u>transported grain from Saskatchewan to Montreal</u>.

_____

 SSR1147   ISBN: 9781771587334 © On The Mark Press

Name: _____

Write the word or words that best complete each sentence.

1. Donnie and _____ are going to the hockey game with dad.
   me / him / I

2. _____ are selling tickets to the school play.
   Me / They / Them

3. The monkeys _____ up the walls of the cage every day.
   climb / is climbing / is jumping

4. Our team _____ 20 players and two coaches.
   has / gots / have

5. _____ a friend to the skating party on Saturday.
   Bringed / Bring / Brought

Name: _____

Bonus Activity: Analogies

Use the correct word from the box to complete each sentence.

1. Happy is to jolly as angry is to _____

2. Claw is to cat as as pincer is to _____

3. Wet is to ocean as dry is to _____

4. Walk is to run as whisper is to_____

5. Milk is to carton as flower is to _____

6. Beef is to cow as pork is to _____

7. Brush is to painter as hammer is to _____

8. Racquet is to tennis as club is to_____

vase
carpenter
shout
annoyed
desert
lobster
pig
caught

MY CANADA *More than 70% of the world's maple syrup is produced in Quebec.*

SSR1147   ISBN: 9781771587334 © On The Mark Press

Tell if these word pairs are *antonyms, homophones,* or *synonyms*.

1. see, look   _____

2. flew, flu   _____

Correct these sentences.

3. ive got a big problem ive lost my jacket said emma

_____

4. please ask aunt lucy if she would like to come for dinner on sunday

_____

Tell if the underlined word is a *noun, pronoun,* or *verb*.

5. Mother <u>opened</u> the jar of peanut butter for me. _____

What the meaning of the underlined figures of speech?

1. <u>Time flew</u> when we were at the water park.

_____

2. That little boy has <u>ants in his pants</u>.

_____

Correct these sentences.

3. has you ever been to the calgary stampede

_____

4. im glad that miss harris is hour jim teacher this year said penny

_____

Write *sentence* or *not a sentence*.

5. The skateboard park _____

 SSR1147   ISBN: 9781771587334 © On The Mark Press

Name: _____

Correct these sentences.

1. the rescue canada helicopter flue right over our house on friday

_____

2. we needs to meet tom at 800 or well be late

_____

Tell whether the underlined word has a *prefix* or a *suffix*.

3. He was <u>careful</u> not to step in the puddle of mud. _____

4. Mom wants to <u>preview</u> that movie before we watch it. _____

In what part of the friendly letter would you find the following word?

5. Dear _____

Name: _____

Number these words in alphabetical order.

1. ___ page   ___ panic   ___ palace   ___ painful   ___ parcel   ___ panda

Correct these sentences.

2. the mechanic told us that our truck is gonna be fixed on tuesday

_____

3. if you dont wate for me i wont be able to go with you

_____

Where would these events likely take place?

4. He shot the puck and scored the winning goal. _____

5. The actors came out on stage for their final bow. _____

Name: _____

Reference sources: atlas, almanac, dictionary, encyclopedia, thesaurus

What reference source would be best to look for information on the following:

1. The location of the St. Lawrence River. _____

2. the highest mountain range in Canada. _____

3. information on Nunavut. _____

4. an antonym for the word "shiny". _____

5. the meaning of the word "aboriginal". _____

Name: _____

Bonus Activity: Sounds Like...

Choose a words from the box that describes how each of these things sound.

| jingle | rustle | crackles | rumbles | honk | hisses | patter | crack | chime |

1. Horns _____   6. Fire _____

2. Raindrops _____   7. Leaves _____

3. Coins _____   8. Coins _____

4. Steam _____   9. Thunder _____

5. Whips _____

Canada has its own mysterious lake creature, Ogopogo.

MY CANADA   *It is reported to live in Lake Okanagan, British Columbia.*

    SSR1147   ISBN: 9781771587334 © On The Mark Press

Name: _____

Correct these sentences.

1. is it gonna snow on thursday or friday asked billy

_____

2. have you ever went skiing at mont tremblant quebec

_____

What is this person probably doing?

3. Grandpa put a worm on his hook and dropped it into the water.

_____

Give a synonym for each word.

4. easy _____

5. cold _____

WEEK
19

ACTIVITY
1

TOTAL
/5

Name: _____

Circle the word that is spelled correctly.

1. oppasit   oppasite   opposite   oposite

Correct these sentences.

2. my coat is missing too buttins it needs to mended too

_____

3. i like sandwiches cookies milk and an apple in my lunch

_____

Present, past or future?

4. Sally learned how to read when she was five years old. _____

5. Mom will paint my room yellow and green. _____

WEEK
19

ACTIVITY
2

TOTAL
/5

SSR1147   ISBN: 9781771587334 © On The Mark Press

Name: _____

Circle the words that have the same sound as the "oo" in "goose".

1. cook   tuna   cupful   fruit   smooth

Is the underlined part the subject or the predicate of the sentence?

2. Uncle Amos <u>rang the doorbell of our house</u>. _____

3. <u>An owl</u> was perched high up on a beam in the barn _____

Correct these sentences.

4. amelia carrie and molly they went shopping with there cousin

_____

5. do you has my number on your sell phone

_____

Name: _____

Who might be saying the following?

1. "Tell me where your arm hurts the most." _____

2. "Tomorrow will be sunny and warm." _____

Circle the word that is spelled correctly.

3. petrafy   petrufy   petrefy   petrify   petrofy

Correct these sentences.

4. how old was you when you loosed you first tooth

_____

5. mom asked did you finished all your homwork last nite

_____

     SSR1147   ISBN: 9781771587334 © On The Mark Press

Name: _____

Explain in your own words the meaning of the underlined figures of speech.

1. My teenage brother <u>eats like a horse</u>.

_____

2. I am going to be <u>in my parents' bad books</u> if I don't find my jacket.

_____

3. My little cousin, Ella, <u>swims like a fish</u>.

_____

4. She <u>goes wild</u> when she hears that group perform.

_____

5. On rainy days, we <u>drive my mom up the wall</u>.

_____

- -

Name: _____

Bonus Activity: Little Words Count

Choose a little word from the box to complete each sentence.

with there by in me up from on too at

1. Andy built the house _____ the creek.

2. Michael is good _____ football.

3. We put our trust _____ the doctor.

4. The dog jumped ____ on the little boy.

5. She does not agree _____ you.

6. We shall count _____ you to do well.

7. Sam is suffering _____ a bad cold.

8. Yesterday it was _____ hot to work.

9. The coats are hanging over _____.

10. Dad gave Jim and ____ some candy.

MY CANADA   *There are approximately 2 million lakes in Canada.*

Name: _____

Complete the analogy.

1. Earth is to planet as Sun is to _____

Give two words that rhyme with each of the following words.

2. handy _____   _____

3. raid _____   _____

Correct these sentences.

4. the january book fair will be held at lincoln park library

_____

5. my sister allison is getting married on sat july 10 2015

_____

Name: _____

Correct these sentences.

1. does you know the name of the boy who moved next door asked grandma

_____

2. basketball practis are changed to wenesday night coach reminded us

_____

Divide each word into syllables.

3. fantastic _____

4. enormous _____

Write a common noun for the proper noun.

5. Toronto Blue Jays _____

SSR1147   ISBN: 9781771587334 © On The Mark Press

Name: _____

Write the correct abbreviations for:

1. Wednesday _____ Thursday _____ Saturday _____

Correct these sentences.

2. his dog hector have ben trained to do for tricks

_____

3. our doctor gived us our flew shot it didnt hert

_____

Write the two words used to make each contraction.

4. shouldn't _____ _____

5. they've _____ _____

Name: _____

Write the root word for each of these words.

1. unreachable _____

2. carelessly _____

Correct these sentences.

3. does you have any water juice or milk in yur fridge that i could has

_____

4. he agreed to do his shar there project gots finished

_____

Circle the word that does not belong.

5. toaster   freezer   microwave   oven

Name: _____

Combine these sentences to make one interesting sentence.

1. My jacket is black. It has my name on it. It has the school crest on it.

    _____

2. My Grandmother is 85. Her birthday is January 7. We are having a party for her.

    _____

3. The truck turned right. It is going to the gas station. The truck is brown.

    _____

4. I have two brothers. They are younger. They are twins.

    _____

5. The truck picks up our garbage. It comes on Thursday. It comes at 7 o'clock.

    _____

- -

Name: _____

Bonus Activity: Action! Action!

Read the words below. Colour the boxes that have words that are verbs.
Hint: you should find 10 words.

king	sprint	trees	whine
rough	rush	bottle	spy
laugh	fast	scatter	dove
tomato	bounce	feet	smile
twist	candy	growl	branches

MY CANADA *Winnipeg, Manitoba is known as the Slurpee Capital of the world.*

SSR1147   ISBN: 9781771587334 © On The Mark Press

Use context clues to explain the meaning of the underlined words.

1. William caught the <u>smelt</u> by using a fine-meshed net.

_____

2. Leaving our friends behind by moving to a new city is a <u>monumental</u> decision for our family.

_____

Correct these sentences.

3. eddie he went to to regina saskatchewan to watch the roughriders play football

_____

4. him and her have the same jacket on today dont they

_____

Write the root word for:

5. removed _____

- -

Correct these sentences.

1. mom gived us a choose between hot dogs or french fires for lunch

_____

2. the movie called the littlest elf is a christmas favourite of me

_____

Give two words that rhyme with each of these words.

3. learn _____ _____

4. him _____ _____

Tell if the pair of words are *synonyms*, *antonyms*, or *homophones*?

5. weight, wait _____ _____

Name: _____

Where would this event probably be happening?

1. Place your items on the counter so the cashier can scan them.

_____

Correct these sentences.

2. me and alice maked up a song for hour play called in the dark forest

_____

3. our school sir winston churchill is the greatest school in nova scotia

_____

Fact or fantasy?

4. We are learning to speak and write in French.   _____

5. The magic beans grew into a giant beanstalk.   _____

Name: _____

Correct these sentences.

1. in grade too i brang my pet hamster ollie to school for show and tell

_____

2. will you poor me a glass of icey cold milk asked teddy

_____

Write the root word for each of these words.

3. unlucky   _____

4. misunderstanding   _____

Write an antonym for this word.

5. same   _____

SSR1147   ISBN: 9781771587334 © On The Mark Press

Name: _____

Reference sources: atlas, almanac, dictionary, encyclopedia, thesaurus

What reference source would be best to look for information on the following:

1. the meaning of the word "fusion" _____

2. the direction you would travel to reach Australia _____

3. what a grizzly bear eats _____

4. the average temperature in Labrador City for a year _____

5. a synonym for the word "tease" _____

Name: _____

Bonus Activity: Chain Words

Read the sentence clues. Think of a word that could fit in the blank. Write the word by putting one letter in each space. One letter has been filled in for you.

1.	She has _____ apple.			n			
2.	Dad cooks eggs in a _____.				n		
3.	Our mother will be home _____ from work.					n	
4.	I love _____ for breakfast.						n
5.	This sandwich is _____ good!	s					
6.	Ships sail across the _____ .	s					
7.	Clothing was cheap at the _____ .	s					

MY CANADA   *The Stanley Cup has its own body guard.*

Name: _____

Fact or opinion?

1. Your music is too loud! _____

2. A tree fell on the roof of our garage. _____

Circle the word that comes first alphabetically.

3. novice   nuclear   next   nasty   notify

Correct these sentences.

4. shawn is going to visit his grandfather last weekend in kelowna british columbia

_____

5. we breaked moms lamp she will be angry at us

_____

Name: _____

Tell how many syllables are in this word.

1. unreliable _____

Write the pronoun for the underlined words.

2. <u>Jerry and Sam</u> live near the library. _____

3. Are you going to the movie with <u>Jane</u>? _____

Correct these sentences.

4. hour flight to from toronto international airport to dawson city left at 800

_____

5. the primary colours are red blue yellow they can be mixed to make new colours

_____

 SSR1147   ISBN: 9781771587334 © On The Mark Press

Name: _____

Circle the words that have three syllables.

1. everywhere   sad   telescope   little   hopefully

2. opening   closing   direction   understand   water

Circle the word that is spelled correctly.

3. froot   friut   fruit   frote   frute

Correct these sentences.

4. chris brang hims comic book collecshun to show hour class

_____

5. my sister dont wanna help me dew my math homework

_____

Name: _____

Tell what this person's job would be.

1. He risks his life to save people from dangerous situations like burning buildings.

_____

Correct these sentences.

2. lets plan a surprise birthday party for dad mom whisperd

_____

3. my uncle henry works at canadas weather station in the arctic

_____

Use context clues to explain the meaning of the underlined words.

4. I don't believe that story. Did you <u>fabricate</u> it?

_____

5. Ron's <u>occupation</u> is driving a school bus for elementary students.

_____

Name: _____

Write the word or words that best complete each sentence.

1. My cousin _____ have any serious allergies.
    don't / does / doesn't

2. We celebrate Valentine's Day on _____ .
    Febrary 14 / February 14 / Feburary 14

3. The basketball player tossed the ball _____ the hoop and scored.
    threw / throw / through

4. Miss Graves _____ a second chance to learn our spelling words.
    gived / gave / given

5. Celia and I _____ dance lessons on Tuesdays after school.
    take / takes / tooks

Name: _____

Bonus Activity: Riddle Me This!

Read the riddle. Choose a word from the box to answer each riddle.

1. I have a face but no eyes. _____

2. I have two banks but no money. _____

3. I have a back and legs but cannot walk. _____

4. I have a lip but no mouth. _____

5. I have teeth but cannot bite. _____

6. I run around your yard but have no legs. _____

7. I have an eye but cannot see. _____

| chair |
| fence |
| needle |
| jug |
| river |
| saw |
| clock |

MY CANADA   *The average Canadian eats 190 eggs per year. Scrambles, anyone?*

   SSR1147   ISBN: 9781771587334 © On The Mark Press

Name: _____

Correct these sentences.

1. who winned the basketball game when you players the raiders

_____

2. did you feeled any presshure to score points for your teem

_____

Use context clues to explain the meaning of the underlined word.

3. She was crying so hard that her words were all <u>garbled</u>.

_____

Circle the word that comes first in alphabetical order.

4. honey   hang   hour   hunger   helicopter

5. stoplight   stony   stove   store   style

Name: _____

Correct these sentences.

1. we swimmed all day at the beech we went tasleeep early

_____

2. abby and sarah are learning to dive they want to be on the swim teem

_____

Present, past or *future*?

3. She went to the store to buy hot dog buns.   _____

4. Tomorrow she is going shopping for new shoes.   _____

Write the contraction made from these two words.

5. should not   _____

Name: _____

Correct these sentences.

1. mr thoms learned us how to make awsome sand castles

_____

2. i didn't expect to saw you out hear so late said my uncle howard

_____

Tell if these words are *synonyms* or *antonyms*.

3. fantastic, terrific   _____

Divide the following words into syllables.

4. attention   _____

5. grandfather   _____

- -

Name: _____

In which part of a friendly letter would the following be found?

1. Your friend, Harry   _____

Give three words that rhyme with each of these words.

2. good   _____

3. gave   _____

Correct these sentences.

4. jake and larry is good friends they is in the same grade too

_____

5. me and janet is going to shopping at the west edmonton mall on friday

_____

SSR1147   ISBN: 9781771587334 © On The Mark Press

Name: _____

Decide if the underlined parts have a *capitalization* error, a *punctuation* error, a *spelling* error or *no mistake*.

1. A firefly is <u>not a true fly but is a beetle.</u> _____

2. <u>In the daytime it is like any other beetle</u> with a brown or black body.

   _____

3. <u>Then at night</u> it becomes a glowing lantern. _____

4. In some countries in <u>africa</u>, people put fireflies in cages. _____

5. <u>Firelies</u> can produce enough light to help you find your way.

   _____

Name: _____

Bonus Activity: Whether the Weather ...

Across
1. On a _____ day you cannot see very far.
2. On a _____ day you might hear thunder.
3. On a _____ day you will need your umbrella.

Down
4. On a _____ day you feel hot and sticky.
5. On a _____ day you should dress warmly.
6. On a _____ day the sky is grey.
7. A _____ day is a good day for a walk.
8. On a _____ day the leaves rustle in the trees.

rainy   mild   cloudy   foggy
stormy   humid   frosty   breezy

Name: _____

Use context to explain the meaning of the underlined word in this sentence.

1. Early explorers needed a good <u>cartographer</u> to provide them with accurate charts and maps.

_____

Correct these sentences.

2. mr howard said tonights homework is to review the chapter on jacques cartier

_____

3. does you got any puppys for sail

_____

Complete the analogies.

4. bird is to sky as fish is to _____

5. lettuce is to green as tomato is to _____

Name: _____

Add a suffix to the following words.

1. hop   _____

2. come   _____

Correct these sentences.

3. does you no what you is doing for your science projeckt

_____

4. ralph is lerning how to play golf with his unckle fred

_____

Tell if this sentence is *interrogative, exclamatory* or *command*.

5. Here comes the first place runner! _____

SSR1147   ISBN: 9781771587334 © On The Mark Press

Name: _____

Give the subject of the following sentence.

1. My friends and I ordered the daily special for our lunch. _____

Correct these sentences.

2. our class went on a field trip to casa loma in toronto on tues may 23 2015

_____

3. everyone loved the ride called the big zipper at the local fare

_____

Write the pronoun that would replace the underlined noun.

4. <u>Mark's model</u> car won first place in the contest. _____

5. Do you know who <u>Ali</u> plays basketball with? _____

Name: _____

Correct these sentences.

1. her and me wanted to prove that we didnt brake moms favourite dish

_____

2. the diver swimmed near the wreck to sea if there were a treasure inside

_____

Write the past tense of each verb.

3. give _____

4. run _____

Tell if the underlined word is a noun, verb or adjective.

5. What time does the adventure movie <u>start</u>? _____

Name: _____

Explain the meaning of the underlined figures of speech.

1. The baseball players were <u>at each others' throats</u> over the rules of the game.

    _____

2. Ella smiled <u>from ear to ear</u> when she won the art contest.

    _____

3. Superman flies faster <u>than a speeding bullet</u>.

    _____

4. Most two - year olds have <u>a mind of their own</u>.

    _____

5. This cold makes me feel like I am <u>in a fog</u>.

    _____

Name: _____

Bonus Activity: Adverbs! dverbs!

Read the words below. Colour the boxes that have words that are adverbs.
Hint: you should find 10 words.

quickly	dinner	roughly	brook
lesson	sleepily	catcher	parade
flag	lazily	tower	brightly
loudly	proudly	angrily	moon
noisily	whistle	team	dimly

MY CANADA

The *world's largest totem pole* was raised in Victoria, British Columbia in 1994.

SSR1147   ISBN: 9781771587334 © On The Mark Press

Correct these sentences.

1. we is trying to memerize the poem indian summer

_____

2. which mall has a movie theatre showing into the deep asked jane

_____

Write the possessive nouns.

3. the shoes of the shoemaker _____

4. the pool of the hotel _____

Write the two words used to make this contraction.

5. She'd _____

Correct these sentences.

1. my favourite nhl teams are the edmonton oilers and the calgary flames

_____

2. my brother andy likes the ottawa senators and the vancouver canucks

_____

Circle the word that comes last in alphabetical order.

3. newborn   newspaper   newt   news   newcomer

How many syllables in each word?

4. Nunavut _____

5. Nova Scotia _____

Name: _____

Simile or metaphor?

1. Wouldn't it be great to fly <u>like a bird</u>? _____

2. The old tree cast a <u>ghostly shadow</u> on the ground. _____

Correct these sentences.

3. our parents announced to the family we is going to visit the yukon in july

_____

4. dad read the story the littlest bear to me and amy at bedtime

_____

Number these words in alphabetical order.

5. _____ elbow   _____ elk   _____ email   _____ elm   _____ elephant

---

Name: _____

Correct these sentences.

1. dad shouted brang me the rope hung on the wall in the shed

_____

2. on saturday michael gave me the book called the lost boy to read

_____

Does the underlined adjective tell *what kind, how many* or *which one*?

3. There are <u>a few</u> cookies left in the cookie jar. _____

Fact or fantasy?

4. The fairy godmother told Cinderella to be home by midnight. _____

5. Walt Disney produced many films about fairy tales. _____

     SSR1147   ISBN: 9781771587334 © On The Mark Press

Name: _____

Reference sources: atlas, almanac, dictionary, encyclopedia, thesaurus

What reference source would be best to look for information on the following:

1. the location of Glacier National Park _____

2. the province with oil as its main export _____

3. the origin of the word "poutine" _____

4. information about the animals living in the Arctic _____

5. a synonym for the word " frigid" _____

Name: _____

Bonus Activity: Dictionary Detective

Check the meaning of each word in the dictionary. Circle the correct meaning.

1. **slink**
   a) to smell
   b) to creep around
   c) to steal

2. **ladle**
   a) a large spoon
   b) a baby's toy
   c) to waddle

3. **voyage**
   a) a trip on horseback
   b) a trip by car
   c) a trip by water

4. **rind**
   a) to look for
   b) a peeling
   c) an African animal

5. **rickety**
   a) noisy
   b) weak and shaky
   c) noise like a cricket

6. **hack**
   a) a bag
   b) to cut by chopping
   c) a type of coat

7. **clash**
   a) to hold tightly
   b) to stick
   c) to hit together noisily

8. **rosy**
   a) a reddish colour
   b) a bunch of flowers
   c) a bunch of horses

9. **dawn**
   a) a baby deer
   b) soft feathers
   c) almost daylight

Name: _____

Present, past, **or** *future?*

1. We're going to the baseball game on Saturday. _____

2. He enjoyed his trip to Halifax last summer. _____

Correct these sentences.

3. betsy said im bringing sandwitches cookies and juise boxes to the picnick

_____

4. i went to the circus on saturday i saw a man hi up on a trapeze

_____

Circle the correct abbreviation for "September".

5. sept   Sep.   Septbr   Sept.   Septem.

Name: _____

Complete the analogies.

1. Brazil is to South America as Canada is to _____

2. apple is to tree as berry is to _____

Divide the word into syllables.

3. disappear   _____

Correct these sentences.

4. uncle bob visit us on his way to regina saskatchewan

_____

5. in june i gets to be in my cousin ashleys wedding

_____

SSR1147   ISBN: 9781771587334 © On The Mark Press

Name: _____

Subject **pronoun or** *object* **pronoun?**

1.   <u>We</u> love to sing the song "The Good Old Hockey Game". _____

2.   The Gradys visited <u>him</u> in Moncton last year.   _____

Correct these sentences.

3.   boys and girls listen for a minute please said our soccer coach

_____

4.   how far is it to kingston from hear asked the tourist

_____

Write the *past* **and the** *future tense* **for the following verb.**

5.   cry   _____   _____

Name: _____

Correct these sentences.

1.   alice goed to the dentist on monday and was gave a new read toothbrush

_____

2.   mr jones were working on his lawnmower he finally gots it fixed

_____

Name the part of speech for the underlined word.

3.   The <u>cruise</u> ship sailed around the Gaspe Peninsula. _____

4.   Jon <u>races</u> his car at the speedway in his town.   _____

Write a good sentences using this pair of homophones.

5.   bear, bare

_____

Name: _____

Combine these sentences into one good sentence.

1. The students debated the topic. The topic was school uniforms. They did not reach a conclusion.

_____

2. Mom got flowers for Mother's Day. They were yellow daffodils. She was surprised.

_____

3. Dad and I went to Pizza Palace. It is on James Street. We had the Super Special.

_____

4. My sundae was made with chocolate ice cream. It had chocolate syrup and sprinkles. It was delicious!

_____

5. I have an awesome pet. It is an iguana. I call him Hector.

_____

Name: _____

Bonus Activity: Name That Place!

Choose a word from the box to complete the sentence.

1. Planks are made from logs at a _____

2. Stone is dug from a _____

3. Cars are made in a _____

4. Bread is baked at a _____

5. Plants are grown and sold at a _____

6. Clothes are washed at a _____

7. Books are stored and loaned from a _____

bakery
factory
library
quarry
laundromat
nursery
sawmill

The Canadian National Exhibition (CNE) was held for the first time on August 3, 1879 in Toronto, Ontario.

MY CANADA

   SSR1147   ISBN: 9781771587334 © On The Mark Press

Name: _____

Correct these sentences.

1. our school vacation begun on june 24 2014 and end on september 4 2014

_____

2. grandpa buyed hot dogs and french fries for us to eat on the annual scouts picnic

_____

Write the two words that make up each contractions.

3. haven't _____   _____

4. would've _____   _____

Write the possessive noun.

5. the colour of the pony _____

Name: _____

Circle the word that is not spelled correctly.

1. dinner   dynamite   disappear   draggon

2. cave   clover   close   culamity

Write the number of syllables in this word.

3. uniforms _____

Correct these sentences.

4. they is moving to a new house at 1427 apple hill lane

_____

5. the leafs blue off the trees and into hour yard

_____

Name: _____

Use context clues to explain the meaning of the underlined words.

1.   Are you buying balloons and streamers for her birthday <u>decorations</u>?

_____

2.   I could not <u>focus</u> on my work because they were singing and laughing.

_____

Correct these sentences.

3.   does you wanna go to see the movie lost land with me asked jared

_____

4.   willys dog buddy chased my cat fuzzy down maple street on sunday

_____

Present, past **or** *future*?

5.   We will see Kurt Browning skate at the All Stars in January. _____

Name: _____

Circle the words that have the same vowel sound as "ay" in "play".

1.   today   donkey   paint   party   they

Correct these sentences.

2.   dean blowed out all twelfe candles on hims birthday cake

_____

3.   my ice cream sunday was covered with syrup berries and peanuts

_____

Write the verb in each sentence.

4.   I read your funny story yesterday.   _____

5.   The doorbell rang four times.   _____

SSR1147   ISBN: 9781771587334 © On The Mark Press

Name: _____

Write the word or words that best complete each sentence.

1. Brandon and _____ are invited to the birthday party.
   I / me

2. The boys had a _____ time at the basketball game.
   well / good

3. Chris drove the car really _____ for a beginner.
   well / good

4. Will you pass _____ the potatoes, please?
   I / me

5. If we play _____ , we will win the championship game.
   well / good

Name: _____

Bonus Activity: When I hear "Canada", I think of...

Find and circle the following words in the puzzle.

S	T	V	O	I	M	F	R	E	L	O	I	N	L
H	R	E	K	M	C	L	M	O	O	S	E	E	S
O	U	C	K	C	D	S	A	N	O	M	O	R	U
C	N	N	T	R	C	M	P	A	N	I	N	O	T
K	O	T	G	E	T	T	L	H	I	R	O	C	U
E	P	O	U	T	I	N	E	G	E	H	W	K	H
Y	A	W	T	A	L	O	L	V	E	L	Y	I	D
A	Y	E	B	T	O	T	E	M	P	O	L	E	S
U	Y	R	A	P	B	E	A	V	E	R	S	R	S O
P	E	R	S	I	V	H	F	O	W	J	D	O	E
P	O	L	A	R	B	E	A	R	S	N	T	C	A

Word list:
RCMP
BEAVER
MOOSE
ROCKIES
CN TOWER
HOCKEY
POLAR BEAR
POUTINE
TOTEM POLES
LOONIE
MAPLE LEAF

Name: _____

Use context to explain the meaning of the underlined word in this sentence.

1. That is a <u>beautiful</u> bouquet of flowers. _____

2. Her skating dress <u>sparkles</u> when she jumps. _____

Correct these sentences.

3. have you ever sang the song god save the queen

_____

4. canada's queen is queen elizabeth II she lives in england

_____

Write the present tense of the verb in this sentence.

5. My dog dug holes in our lawn. _____

Name: _____

Where would the following probably take place?

1. After a great ride down, we had to walk back up the hill.

_____

Correct these sentences.

2. jacksons baseball team has too outs and too strike

_____

3. we is going to have a visit from sparky the fire safety dog tomorrow

_____

***Fact* or *fiction*?**

4. Corduroy the bear lost the button off his overalls. _____

5. Grizzly bears can be very dangerous to humans. _____

     SSR1147   ISBN: 9781771587334 © On The Mark Press

Name: _____

In which part of a friendly letter would you find the following?

1. I hope we can go swimming while I am there. _____

2. Your cousin, Sally _____

Where would someone probably say the following?

3. Would you like fries with your burger? _____

Correct these sentences.

4. he ride a mountain bike that gots red flames

_____

5. the baby robin weighted for it's mother to brang it a worm

_____

Name: _____

Complete the analogy.

1. multiplication is to division as addition is to _____

Correct these sentences.

2. were saving monay by using hour coupons to by food and other things

_____

3. she dont like the taste of chockolit but she do like strawberry

_____

Where would the following probably take place?

4. We stopped when the light turned red and waited for the green light.

_____

5. Mother is scrambling some eggs for us to eat.

_____

Decide if the underlined parts have a *capitalization* error, a *punctuation* error, a *spelling* error or *no mistake*.

1. <u>polar</u> bears are excellent swimmers.   _____

2. They can <u>stay underwater for up to two minutes.</u> _____

3. A polar <u>bears</u> sense of smell is very strong. _____

4. It can <u>cents</u> a whale from 20 miles away. _____

5. Polar bears like to eat <u>whales seals and walruses.</u> _____

Bonus Activity: Buzz! Flutter! Fly!

Write the correct name of these insects to complete the sentence.

1. A _____ sucks blood.

2. The _____ makes honey.

3. A _____ sings in the summer.

4. A _____ glows in the dark of night.

5. A _____ has spots on its back.

6. A _____ flies at night.

7. The _____ is brightly coloured.

8. If a _____ stings you, it will hurt.

| cricket |
| moth |
| butterfly |
| mosquito |
| ladybug |
| wasp |
| firefly |
| bee |

 SSR1147   ISBN: 9781771587334 © On The Mark Press

Name: _____

Correct these sentences.

1. are class maid a graph to show information about favourite plce to visit in canada

_____

2. moms car breaked down on her weigh home so she called a toe truck

_____

Singular or *plural* **noun?**

3. teeth _____

4. toothbrush _____

Write the two words used to make this contraction.

5. I'm _____

Name: _____

Correct these sentences.

1. him and her have the leed parts in the play anne of green gables

_____

2. jeff the whether man gave us the long range forcast for victoria british columbia

_____

Use context clues to explain the meaning of the underlined words.

3. The aroma of hot chocolate floated through the arena.

_____

4. Chloe was ecstatic when she won the first prize of $100.

_____

Is this sentence *exclamatory*, *interrogative*, **a** *statement* **or a** *command*?

5. Have you ever visited the Toronto Metro Zoo? _____

Name: _____

Correct these sentences.

1. in banff alberta we gots to go sking with hour unckle george

_____

2. we will fed the sheep after we groom the hoarse said tom

_____

Common or proper noun?

3. Nahanni National Park   _____

4. campfire   _____

Write the adjectives in this sentence.

5. Who is the girl wearing the red and black dress?   _____

Name: _____

Write the root or base word for these words.

1. confusion   _____

2. swimming   _____

Correct these sentences.

3. the spectaters clapped loud when he scored the wining goal

_____

4. miss vogel said we will have the final test in history on thursday january 30

_____

Divide this word into syllables.

5. vacation   _____

    SSR1147   ISBN: 9781771587334 © On The Mark Press

Name: _____

Explain the meaning of the underlined figure of speech.

1. <u>Were your ears burning</u> when you heard we were talking about your new bike?

_____

2. We knew we were <u>in a jam</u> when the canoe tipped over.

_____

3. Miss Griffin was <u>singing your praises</u> for setting up the Science Fair.

_____

4. You will do a great job in the play. <u>Break a leg</u>!

_____

5. We cannot play outside because it is <u>raining cats and dogs</u>.

_____

_____

Name: _____

Bonus Activity: Animal Unscramble

Unscramble these words to correctly spell the names of Canadian animals.

1. lowf

_____

2. ralop raeb

_____

3. erd fxo

_____

4. biracuo

_____

5. xnyl

_____

6. zzylgir raeb

_____

7. mpchiknu

_____

8. ffolaub

_____

The Montreal Canadiens played their first game in their new home – the Forum – and won on November 29, 1924.

MY CANADA

Write the two words that make this contraction.

1. he'll   _____

Correct these sentences.

2. ava is gonna borrow graces blew dress for the party on saturday

_____

3. evan ted and grant went with there dad to by knew bikes

_____

Circle the word that is spelled correctly.

4. breekfast   brekfast   breakfast   breckfast

5. ellbow   elbo   eelbow   elbow

Opinion or fact?

1. The mildest soap to use on your face is Dove. _____

Correct these sentences.

2. miss leader mrs martin and mr cummings all teach at hartford elementary school

_____

3. sarh and louis taked pictures of animals at granby zoo

_____

Write number of syllables in each word.

4. situation   _____

5. demolition   _____

SSR1147   ISBN: 9781771587334 © On The Mark Press

Correct these sentences.

1. i just finished reading a book called emily of new moon by l m montgomery

_____

2. may i borrow your ruler and eraser alex whispered

_____

Complete the analogy.

3. yesterday is to past as tomorrow is to _____

Number these words in alphabetical order.

4. ___ clover   ___ cleaver   ___ clean   ___ clam   ___ clump

5. ___ marsh   ___ mind   ___ mention   ___ many   ___ mood

Correct these sentences.

1. i dont have no time to waste im late shouted quentin

_____

2. i've picked up a nail in my knew tyre exclaimed mrs foster

_____

Present , past, **or** *future.*

3. Shawn flew his remote airplane in the big field. _____

Name the part of speech for the underlined word.

4. The bus left <u>promptly</u> at 7:30 a.m. _____

5. Jacob <u>bounced</u> the basketball twice , then shot it. _____

Reference sources: atlas, almanac, dictionary, encyclopedia, thesaurus

What reference source would be best to look for information on the following:

1. the location of the Baffin Island _____

2. the number of syllables in the word "confederation" _____

3. information on Polar Bear Provincial Prk _____

4. an antonym for the word "gloom" _____

5. the meaning of the word "antique" _____

WEEK
30

ACTIVITY
5

TOTAL
/5

Name: _____

WEEK
30

Bonus Activity: Yum! Poutine!

Poutine is a favourite treat for many Canadians. Here are some words related to poutine. **Write the words under the correct heading.**

BONUS!
ACTIVITY

cheese gravy curds bowl gooey tasty fries messy poutine Canadian

One Syllable Words	Two Syllable Words	Four Syllable Words

John McCrae's poem "In Flanders Fields" was first published on December 8, 1915.

MY CANADA

SSR1147   ISBN: 9781771587334 © On The Mark Press

Name: _____

Circle the word that is spelled correctly.

1. neccessary   neccesary   necessary   necessery

2. begining   beginning   beggining   begning

Correct these sentences.

3. fred falled on the ice he broke his write wrist

_____

4. in february we have spirit week at blackburn middle school

_____

Write the past tense for this verb.

5. cry   _____

- -

Name: _____

Opinion or fact?

1. Maple syrup tastes great on vanilla ice cream.   _____

2. Quebec produces a great deal of Canada's maple syrup. _____

Correct these sentences.

3. how many books did you reed this summer asked the librarian

_____

4. does you want to go toboganning with us on big ben hill

_____

Underline the cause and circle the effect in this sentence.

5. The traffic light turned green, so we walked across the street.

Name: _____

Write a good sentence for each pair of antonyms.

1. wealthy, poor

_____

2. hardworking, lazy

_____

Present, past or future?

3. Gus will meet us at the movies. _____

Correct these sentences.

4. he called max his best friend to find out the time of the game

_____

5. will you deliver this package for me mr woods asked

_____

Name: _____

Does the adjective tell *what kind, which one,* or *how many*?

1. Nicholas got a reward for finding Ella's lost kitten. _____

Correct these sentences.

2. jen and beth neded a our to get ready for the party

_____

3. you're grandparents live to far away to visit very offen dont they

_____

Opinion or fact?

4. Canada is the greatest country in the world. _____

5. The capital of Canada is Ottawa. _____

SSR1147 ISBN: 9781771587334 © On The Mark Press

Name: _____

Combine these sentences into one good sentence.

1. The score in the game was very close. It was 5 to 4. We won.

_____

2. That test was easy. I studied for two hours. I studied last night.

_____

3. We visited the science museum. It is new. It shows the history of technology.

_____

4. It rained hard all day. The streets were flooded. Some cars got stuck.

_____

5. Penny dove into the pool. She held her breath. She swam underwater.

_____

Name: _____

Bonus Activity: Follow That Adjective!

Follow the path from the START square to the FINISH square by colouring in the boxes that contain adjectives.

START	present	heavy	sunny	strong
deep	joke	green	star	small
red	pretty	cold	dust	powerful
shirt	trousers	books	contest	huge
baby	puppy	brain	creek	FINISH

MY CANADA

Roberta Bondar, first Canadian female astronaut, blasted into space aboard the space shuttle Discovery on January 22, 1992.

SSR1147 ISBN: 9781771587334 © On The Mark Press

Name: _____

Correct these sentences.

1. tim and peggy is getting married and moving to cornerbrook newfoundland

_____

2. how many times does you want me to tell you this story mom asked

_____

Circle the word that comes first in alphabetical order.

3. sparkle   spade   spatter   space   spaniel

Write an antonym for each word.

4. messy   _____

5. early   _____

Name: _____

Where would the following probably take place?

1. We pushed the button for our floor number and the door closed.

_____

Correct these sentences.

2. the blizzard begun at 730 am and ended at 230 pm

_____

3. before you began to cook gather all your ingredients and utinsels

_____

Opinion or *fact*?

4. Visiting a colony of puffins would be great! _____

5. Upper Canada Village shows life in pioneer times. _____

SSR1147 ISBN: 9781771587334 © On The Mark Press

Name: _____

Write the comparative and superlative forms of these adjectives.

1. messy _____

2. good _____

Correct these sentences.

3. grandmas group of frends meet at tim hortons every tuesday mourning

_____

4. him and me got payed for shovelling snow at mrs fletchers house

_____

Circle the correct way to divide this word onto syllables.

5. litt – er – bug   lit – ter – bug   li – tter – bug

Name: _____

Underline the subject in this sentence.

1. The baby laughed when the toy squeaked.

Correct these sentences.

2. dr franklin is a good dentist she is very careful

_____

3. they well name there baby bella if it is a girl patrick if it is a boy

_____

Complete the analogies.

4. strawberry is to red as banana is to _____

5. evening is to dinner as morning is to _____

Write the word or words that best complete each sentence.

1. Which _____ did you take in the debate?
   sighed / side

2. Can we _____ to the middle of the pond?
   wade / weighed

3. If we are going to sell cookies, we want to make a _____.
   prophet / profit

4. Rosa _____ a bright red ribbon in her hair to match her dress.
   war / wore

5. Tyler's black lab had _____ puppies on Sunday.
   eight / ate

Name: _____

Bonus Activity: A Not–So–Secret Message!

Discover the message by writing the letters in the boxes. Write the letter that comes before each one you see. The first one has been done to help you.

C												!
d	b	o	b	e	b	j	t	h	s	f	b	u

Write your own list of three things that make Canada a great place to live!

1. _____

2. _____

3. _____

Barbara Ann Scott won Canada's first Olympic gold in women's figure skating in 1948.

MY CANADA

SSR1147   ISBN: 9781771587334 © On The Mark Press

ANSWER KEY

WEEK 1: ACTIVITY 1

1. Have you ever been to Niagara Falls, Ontario?
2. My friend Nicole lives in Montreal Quebec.
3. 4-buffalo   2-beaver   1-bear   3-bison
4. 4-elm   3-elk   1-eagle   2-eel
5. french fries

WEEK 1: ACTIVITY 2

1. not a sentence
2. sentence
3. My teacher said that we are going to visit the Royal Canadian Mint in Ottawa.
4. Don't you agree that Canadians are the greatest hockey players?
5. proper noun

WEEK 1: ACTIVITY 3

1. Overwhelmed, amazed
2. Our family is going to visit an old Viking settlement in Newfoundland.
3. Wouldn't it be fun to pan for gold in Dawson City in the Yukon?
4. mapel   oake
5. cardonal   eagel

WEEK 1: ACTIVITY 4

1. pi – on – eer
2. Sask – at – chew – an
3. "Have you ever been to the CN Tower?" asked Chloe.
4. Our teacher read the story called White Fang by Jack London
5. P.O.

WEEK 1: ACTIVITY 5

1. gone
2. finish
3. She's
4. has
5. parked

BONUS ACTIVITY:

Answers will vary.

WEEK 2: ACTIVITY 1

1. They get lots of snow in northern Manitoba.
2. The winners of the Stanley Cup will have their team photo on television.
3. does not
4. she will, she shall
5. synonym

WEEK 2: ACTIVITY 2

1. salutation, greeting
2. address
3. fantasy
4. A train ride through the Rocky Mountains would be a great adventure.
5. What a terrific save my friend Charlie made during the soccer tournament!

WEEK 2: ACTIVITY 3

1. explain
2. Have you heard the story of how the Bluenose won her first race?
3. Caribou, beaver, and the polar bear appear on Canadian coins.
4. Canadian provinces
5. Canadian NHL hockey teams

WEEK 2: ACTIVITY 4

1. "Will you be our master of ceremonies for the school concert?" asked Miss Dunn.
2. "I would love to meet my penpal from Nunavut," said Reese.
3. Soak in stain remover.
4. coffee shop
5. snowmobile

WEEK 2: ACTIVITY 5

1. atlas
2. thesaurus
3. encyclopedia
4. dictionary
5. almanac

SSR1147   ISBN: 9781771587334 © On The Mark Press

BONUS ACTIVITY: THE WORD ABOUT BIRDS!

1. robin
2. mallard duck
3. pigeon
4. loon
5. swan
6. vulture

WEEK 3: ACTIVITY 1

1. Amanda's dog had eight puppies last Saturday.
2. "How many spelling words did you get right on your test?" asked Dad.
3. geese: plural
4. foxes: plural
5. enough   rough

WEEK 3: ACTIVITY 2

1. sentence
2. not a sentence
3. We laughed when we heard the story about Paul Bunyan making the Thousand Islands
4. Travelling through the Arctic Ocean could be dangerous.
5. beautiful; red; white; red

WEEK 3: ACTIVITY 3

1. names of Canadian birds
2. flavours of ice cream
3. Vicky asked, "How was your visit with your grandmother?"
4. My grandfather was a fisherman in the waters of the Grand Banks.
5. think: thought

WEEK 3: ACTIVITY 4

1. noun
2. verb
3. "Make sure you come to the players' meeting on Thursday," said the coach.
4. I need to buy new cleats if I am going to play soccer this year.
5. tale / tail   Answers will vary.

WEEK 3: ACTIVITY 5

1. They were very poor.
2. He can run really fast.
3. You look great!
4. He was talking really fast.
5. Time dragged along.

BONUS ACTIVITY: GENDER WORDS

1. grandfather: grandmother   2. husband: wife
3. father: mother   4. brother: sister   5. son: daughter
6. king: queen   7. nephew: niece   8. uncle: aunt

WEEK 4: ACTIVITY 1

1. Have you ever gone skating on the Rideau Canal in Ottawa, Ontario?
2. You can buy hot chocolate, doughnuts and beaver tails at the Canal rink
3. practice
4. hockey / lacrosse / soccer
5. St. John's / Windsor

WEEK 4: ACTIVITY 2

1. slowly / softly
2. knives
3. men
4. Harry is the best friend that I have ever had.
5. Don't you wish we could go to the Quebec Winter Carnival?

WEEK 4: ACTIVITY 3

1. simile
2. not a simile
3. Mack and I do not get to walk to school together.
4. Ellen and her family have gone camping in Algonquin National Park.
5. peso

WEEK 4: ACTIVITY 4

1. bi – son
2. Al – bert – a
3. The puffin is Newfoundland and Labrador's official bird.
4. We saw a tall wooden lighthouse at Peggy's Cove in Nova Scotia.
5. NWT

SSR1147   ISBN: 9781771587334 © On The Mark Press

WEEK 4: ACTIVITY 5

1. encyclopedia
2. almanac
3. atlas
4. dictionary
5. encyclopedia

BONUS ACTIVITY: CANADA'S CAPITALS

Saskatchewan – Regina
Newfoundland – St. Johns
Nova Scotia – Halifax
Ontario – Toronto
Nunavut – Iqaluit
Manitoba – Winnipeg
Alberta – Edmonton
British Columbia – Victoria
Quebec – Quebec City
Yukon – Whitehorse
New Brunswick – Fredericton
NWT – Yellowknife
PEI – Charlottetown

WEEK 5: ACTIVITY 1

1. (Because the was big snowfall), skiing was great!
2. My friend, Joe, lives in Winnipeg with his parents, Max and Ruby.
3. Where would you go to catch a fresh lobster for your dinner?
4. a bear's salmon
5. Mr. Brown's telephone

WEEK 5: ACTIVITY 2

1. 2–ski   4–stroll   5–swim   3–sprint   1–saunter
2. 2–leaf   5–luck   3–light   1–lamp   4–love
3. Mom's plane landed right on time at Toronto International Airport.
4. I can't wait to go to my friend's house in Nova Scotia this summer.
5. swimming in the ocean: Answers will vary.

WEEK 5: ACTIVITY 3

1. scary   scarier   scariest
2. funny   funnier   funniest
3. Fact
4. Walk through this forest and smell the pine trees.
5. "You've made a great presentation on your project," said Mr. Hartley.

WEEK 5: ACTIVITY 4

1. (Dad forgot to set his alarm), so he was late for work.
2. Molly's birthday party will start at 2:00 p.m.
3. Say, did you know that Canada is the second largest country in the world?
4. sleep is to night as work is to day
5. bite is to dog as sting is to bee

WEEK 5: ACTIVITY 5

Answers may vary. Suggestions:
1. Bob and I had fun fishing in Lake Erie.
2. We baked chocolate chip cookies for our school's bake sale.
3. We went to see the Musical Ride where Mounties ride on horses that keep time to the music.
4. Marilyn Bell was only 16 years old when she became the first person to swim across Lake Ontario.
5. Jason wants to go with me to the movies but his mother said he couldn't go.

BONUS ACTIVITY: JUST FOR FUN: HOMONYMS

1. tail / tale   2. maid / made   3. fare / fair   4. deer / dear
5. bean / been   6. male / mail   7. great / grate
8. road / rode

WEEK 6: ACTIVITY 1

1. Dan's father have been transferred to an Armed Forces Base in the Arctic.
2. Were you asleep when I came home last night?
3. ladies
4. shelves
5. knowledge

WEEK 6: ACTIVITY 2

1. low / slow / grow / row
2. Going out to shovel snow.
3. Telling the student to begin a test.
4. Watch out! That car is not stopping for the red light!
5. We got Grandma her favourite cookbook, Holiday Baking, at the bookstore.

WEEK 6: ACTIVITY 3

1. Someone who studies reptiles and amphibians.
2. building a snow fort. Answers may vary.
3. climbing a mountain. Answers will vary.
4. Did you know that the telephone were invented by Alexander Graham Bell?
5. Sam broke the lock and now he doesn't have any way to lock the door on his room.

WEEK 6: ACTIVITY 4

1. Bill, Anna, and Jasmine are in Grade Four at Sir Winston Churchill Public School.
2. Ali told her mother that she were going roller-blading in the park with us.
3. his
4. they
5. Answers will vary.

WEEK 6: ACTIVITY 5

1. Do you want to come shopping at the mall with us?
2. Chelsea gave the bookmark she made to her.
3. The buttons on my sweater are falling off.
4. Grandma's favourite TV show comes on at 2 o'clock.
5. Dad was typing on his laptop in his office.

BONUS ACTIVITY: WORDS FROM NATIVE LANGUAGES

1. acanoe
2. asquash
3. moccasin
4. Winnipeg
5. Miramichi
6. kayak

WEEK 7: ACTIVITY 1

1. Wear warm clothes if you are going tobogganing at Big Hill Park.
2. French fries, gravy, and cheese curds are used to make poutine, a favourite Canadian treat.
3. find / found
4. give / gave
5. Fact

WEEK 7: ACTIVITY 2

1. tooth / teeth
2. canary / canaries
3. The huge ice-breaker slowly made a path for the smaller ships. In the Arctic Ocean
4. My favourite NHL team, the Montreal Canadiens are playing in the Montreal Forum tonight.
5. Robert Munsch has written more than forty books for children.

WEEK 7: ACTIVITY 3

1. unhappy / sad / miserable
2. Mrs. Long said, "Study all 20 words for your spelling test on Friday."
3. Do you believe that Winnipeg is one of the coldest cities in Canada?
4. names of fish
5. winter sports equipment

WEEK 7: ACTIVITY 4

1. When Adam broken his leg he got to use crutches to get around.
2. Mrs. Burns said, "Please sit quietly during the assembly in the gym."
3. Simile
4. the buffalo's horns
5. the bear's claws

WEEK 7: ACTIVITY 5

1. spelling
2. punctuation
3. punctuation
4. capitalization
5. no error

BONUS ACTIVITY: ANAGRAMS

1. pal   2. bad   3. sack   4. dew   5. seal   6. barn   7. deaf

WEEK 8: ACTIVITY 1

1. Saskatchewan has the most roads in all of Canada.
2. "Did you know that ringette and 5-pin bowling were invented by Canadians?" asked Dad.
3. would not
4. they are
5. intention

SSR1147   ISBN: 9781771587334 © On The Mark Press

Week 8: Activity 2

1. wing is to bird as arm is to person
2. run is to horse as fly is to bird
3. January
4. We recited the poem <u>The Cremation of Sam McGee</u> by Robert Service.
5. Our plane made an emergency landing in Gander, Newfoundland.

Week 8: Activity 3

1. proper noun
2. common noun
3. Do you know the words to the song "God Save the Queen"?
4. Our library has many good books about Canadian explorers.
5. Command

Week 8: Activity 4

1. "My mom works as a nurse at the Hotel Dieu Hospital," I told my friend Amy.
2. Sometimes Canada is called "Hollywood North."
3. Betty's telephone line was busy when I tried to call.
4. 3–golf   4–gong   2–going   5–gorilla   1–goat
5. 5–hardly   3–hanging   4–happy   1–hand   2–handsome

Week 8: Activity 5

1. Be brave
2. An excellent view
3. Really hard
4. Sore throat
5. Be very angry

Bonus Activity: Same Category

1. wheat / barley / oats: corn
2. spring / summer / winter: autumn
3. raccoon / moose / buffalo: otter
4. lily / carnation / pansy: daisy
5. football / baseball / hockey: tennis
6. banana / cherry / plum: mango
7. trousers / vest / shirt: jacket

Week 9: Activity 1

1. Simile
2. Metaphor
3. We sang "Soldiers and Sailors" at our Remembrance Day Service.
4. Canada shares four of the Great Lakes with its neighbour, the United States.
5. (Jerry) <u>filled</u> the can with gas for the lawnmower.

Week 9: Activity 2

1. repaint
2. unaware
3. Subject pronoun
4. "Nathan, where is the puppy's leash?" asked Barb.
5. Our cat, Bubbles, loves to sharpen her claws on the scratching post.

Week 9: Activity 3

1. predict
2. The Sledgehammer Ride at Canada's Wonderland is one of a kind.
3. Many children played beside the creek and in the mud.
4. peanut butter: 4
5. polar bear: 3

Week 9: Activity 4

1. We were studying Jacques Cartier in Mr. Roberts' class.
2. I asked my brother, "Do you want to go visit Grandma on Friday?"
3. Dark, cloudy, like rain
4. Subject pronoun
5. Predicate pronoun

Week 9: Activity 5

1. Brad and I play on the same baseball team.
2. Sandy drove the car well.
3. If our team plays well, then we will win the championship.
4. Will you pass me the cookies?
5. Everyone had a good time at the birthday party.

Bonus Activity: Something Fishy!

1. eel   2. bass   3. spawn   4. scales   5. nets   6. gills
7. sardines   8. salmon

WEEK 10: ACTIVITY 1

1. actor 2. their
3. I sat by myself on the bus and slept all the way to Sault Ste. Marie.
4. I read four chapters in my book while I was waiting for you.
5. Beef is to cow as pork is to pig.

WEEK 10: ACTIVITY 2

1. read: unreadable
2. plan: preplanning
3. Opinion
4. I think you were absent when we voted for class president.
5. John McCrae wrote the well known poem, "In Flanders Fields."

WEEK 10: ACTIVITY 3

1. 1–famous 4–fuzzy 3–friendly 2–faster
2. My teacher, Miss Grant , came to our house for dinner last Sunday .
3. Ella, Emily, and Elizabeth went skiing in Quebec last Saturday.
4. noisy / noisier / noisiest
5. sunny / sunnier / sunniest

WEEK 10: ACTIVITY 4

1. Don't give up when you first can't solve the problem.
2. We sing the songs "Jingle Bells" and "Frosty the Snowman" in December.
3. Answers will vary.
4. British Columbia: 6
5. Athabasca: 4

WEEK 10: ACTIVITY 5

1. After I chopped the wood, I carried it into the house and lit the fire.
2. Before Dan went on holidays, he packed his suitcases and put his things in his car.
3. Mom baked a cake in the oven and then she decorated it with sprinkles.
4. I put on my pyjamas, went to bed and read my book.
5. After Dad painted my room with the paint he bought, he admired his work.

BONUS ACTIVITY: COLLECTIVE NOUNS

1. a list of names
2. a pile of wood
3. a herd of cows
4. a pack of cards
5. a set of dishes
6. a school of fish
7. a flock of birds
8. a bale of hay

WEEK 11: ACTIVITY 1

1. Don't you wish we could go to an NHL hockey game in Edmonton?
2. Even though we"d be late for school, we decided to wait for Nathan.
3. Dan lost it on the way to the candy store.
4. She told the class to remember to study for the test.
5. past

WEEK 11: ACTIVITY 2

1. car – i – bou
2. for – tress
3. I told Harry that I was visiting my cousins in Fredericton during Christmas break.
4. My Uncle Hank loves his Ford truck but my aunt drives a Dodge.
5. possible

WEEK 11: ACTIVITY 3

1. Our family left Toronto when my dad got a new job in Winnipeg.
2. Sam, Steve, and I have gone to soccer camp for two years.
3. enormous: huge, gigantic, large
4. puny: skinny, scrawny, thin
5. Waitress

WEEK 11: ACTIVITY 4

1. fact
2. fiction
3. My class is doing an exchange visit with a school in Montreal.
4. Icebergs can be seen off the coast of Newfoundland in April and May.
5. metaphor

SSR1147 ISBN: 9781771587334 © On The Mark Press

WEEK 11: ACTIVITY 5

1. When we went fishing we <u>caught</u> five big fish.
2. Of all the places I have been, I liked Niagara Falls the <u>best</u>.
3. My family have <u>gone</u> to a cottage every July.
4. <u>They're</u> going to wish that they had come to this party.
5. Victor <u>leads</u> the team for the most points in this game.

BONUS ACTIVITY: JOIN TO MAKE ONE WORD

1. nobody
2. eyelid
3. broomstick
4. grasshopper
5. paintbrush
6. nightgown
7. butterfly
8. landslide
9. rooftop
10. campground

WEEK 12: ACTIVITY 1

1. The clouds in the sky were marshmallows floating by.
   – metaphor
2. Mr. Evans said, "I would like to thank Carla and Chris for helping (to) organize Fun Day."
3. Our basketball team is going try hard to win the championship.
4. <u>Her</u> van can carry seven people.
5. <u>It</u> will be here at 1o'clock sharp.

WEEK 12: ACTIVITY 2

1. Do you like chocolate or vanilla ice cream the most?
2. Uncle Peter owns a bait shop on the shore of Lake Erie.
3. tall / taller / tallest
4. strong stronger / strongest
5. opinion

WEEK 12: ACTIVITY 3

1. "Give me all your money," the robber growled.
2. "Help! Help!" screamed the little old lady.
3. We looked for our mitts and found <u>them</u> in the closet. – object
4. object
5. crispy / crispier / crispiest

WEEK 12: ACTIVITY 4

1. When Mario buys his new camera, he will take our picture.
2. The sky turned dark and it began to pour rain.
3. fiction   4. fact
5. adjective

WEEK 12: ACTIVITY 5

1. Punctuation error
2. Spelling error.
3. Spelling error
4. Capitalization error
5. No error

BONUS ACTIVITY: ANIMAL FATHERS AND MOTHERS

1. A mother chicken is a <u>hen</u>.   2. A father duck is a <u>drake</u>.
3. A mother lion is a <u>lioness</u>.   4. A mother pig is a <u>sow</u>.
5. A mother horse is a <u>mare</u>.   6. A father goose is a <u>gander</u>
7. A mother sheep is a <u>ewe</u>.   8. A mother deer is a <u>doe</u>.
9. A mother billy goat is a <u>nanny</u>.   10. A father cow is a <u>bull</u>.

WEEK 13: ACTIVITY 1

1. they're
2. "Excuse me, Miss. How much does this chair cost?" asked Mrs. Peterson.
3. Miss Abbott reminded us, "Study for your test tomorrow."
4. <u>It</u> has run out of gas.
5. Darlene eats lunch with <u>her</u> everyday at school.

WEEK 13: ACTIVITY 2

1. Bill is to William as Bob is to Robert
2. Beth is to Elizabeth as Susie is to Susan
3. On July 1, 1867, Canada became a country.
4. Johnny has broken his bicycle chain so he'll ask his dad to fix it.
5. tale, tail – Answers will vary.

WEEK 13: ACTIVITY 3

1. eagle / eleven / erosion / error / escort / evening
2. Is she saving seats for her four friends at the movie?
3. The boys are helping their grandfather plant his garden on Saturday.
4. must not
5. they have

WEEK 13: ACTIVITY 4

1. m
2. "My favourite yellow flower is a daffodil," said mother.
3. Dad asked, "Did you hear my cellphone ring?"
4. past
5. future

WEEK 13: ACTIVITY 5

1. Not very much fun at all.
2. Thinking very hard.
3. "Be mean; speak crossly.
4. By memory.
5. Was sad.

BONUS ACTIVITY: WORDS! ABOUT OUR BODIES

1. Our teeth grow in our gums.
2. Arms and legs are called limbs.
3. Sweat comes from the pores in our skin.
4. The heart pumps blood around the body.
5. Holes in our noses are called nostrils.
6. The ribs protect our lungs and chest.
7. Bones move at the joints.
8. A cavity is a decaying hole in a tooth.

WEEK 14: ACTIVITY 1

1. My sister and I fell asleep while watching the movie, Frozen.
2. Because the sign said it was 300 kilometres to Toronto, we knew it would be a long trip.
3. Man – i – to – ba
4. caribou
5. muskrat

WEEK 14: ACTIVITY 2

1. Do these two loads of laundry and then put your clothes away in your room.
2. "Try to make your work neater, Jack," said Mrs. Blake.
3. time   Answers will vary.
4. meet   Answers will vary.
5. snow / blow / grow

WEEK 14: ACTIVITY 3

1. you have
2. he will
3. Jill and I went to buy a birthday present for Emily.
4. Her birthday is on Friday, November 13, and her party is on Saturday.
5. homophones

WEEK 14: ACTIVITY 4

1. They like to eat cereal and toast for breakfast each morning.
2. He lost some of his socks so now he wears mismatched pairs.
3. He has to be at work by 7:30 each morning.
4. They marched to the beat of the drum.
5. You should be certain of your facts before making such a serious accusation. A statement that a person has done something wrong or committed a crime.

WEEK 14: ACTIVITY 5

1. almanac
2. thesaurus
3. atlas
4. encyclopedia
5. dictionary

BONUS ACTIVITY: DICTIONARY DETECTIVE

1. sugarcane
2. winter
3. cotton
4. four
5. $2.00
6. French fries, cheese, gravy
7. nothing

WEEK 15: ACTIVITY 1

1. rough / rougher / roughest
2. rocky / rockier / rockiest
3. Sat.
4. "Well, that job was easy when you helped me," I told my sister.
5. We heard a loud noise when the tire blew apart.

SSR1147   ISBN: 9781771587334 © On The Mark Press

Week 15: Activity 2

1. <u>They</u> are going away for the weekend.
2. Did you see the TV special called <u>Atlantic Marine Life</u> on Sunday?
3. Tourists like to take a cruise on the Rideau Canal in July and August.
4. fox / foxes
5. bunch / bunches

Week 15: Activity 3

1. not a sentence
2. gi – gan - tic
3. sol - diers
4. "I'm allergic to peanuts, tree nuts, and walnuts," Chloe said.
5. Tim is looking for a summer job at Jordan's Garden Centre.

Week 15: Activity 4

1. woman / women
2. tooth / teeth
3. "I'm sorry that I can't go with you to the Quebec Winter Carnival," Emma said.
4. Address those small envelopes and then mail them right away.
5. soon   Answers will vary.

Week 15: Activity 5

1. capitalization   2. spelling   3. punctuation
4. capitalization   5. no error

Bonus Activity: Nouns! Nouns! Everywhere!

Boxes that have nouns: canoe, kayak, sea-doo, sailboat, steamer, ferry, scow, sloop
What category do these nouns fit into? Names of ways to travel on water.

Week 16: Activity 1

1. skillfully
2. verb
3. noun
4. We are going camping in Algonquin Park with our neighbours, the Browns.
5. "The Calgary Stampede is a great tourist attraction," said my Uncle Rex.

Week 16: Activity 2

1. opinion
2. give   Answers will vary.
3. stone   Answers will vary.
4. You could join our club if you are able to keep secrets.
5. Dodi said, "I want to be a pilot when I grow up."

Week 16: Activity 3

1. a – gree – ment
2. walk – ing
3. point   Answers will vary.
4. Jane received the Most Valuable Player award for the season.
5. We had hamburgers, french fries, and cookies for dinner on Friday.

Week 14: Activity 4

1. We have to get our bedrooms cleaned up before mom gets home.
2. Do you ride a bus to school or do your parents drive you there?
3. Steve Nash – proper
4. glacier – common
5. churches

Week 16: Activity 5

1. Because deserts are hot places, certain plants cannot grow well.
2. Very little rain falls and then the sun and wind dry it up.
3. Cactus and small bushes grow in the desert.
4. You can see sand for miles and sometimes you see rocks.
5. The desert is such a harsh place that very few people live there.

Bonus Activity: Water Word Search

									r
									e
	o			r	a	p	i	d	s
	c	a	n	a	l				e
	e				d				r
w	a	t	e	r	f	a	l	l	v
	n		b		m			a	o
		a						k	i
	y			r	i	v	e	r	

Week 17: Activity 1

1. She and I left for school at the same time this morning.
2. That's the scariest story I've ever read," said Polly.
3. unpleasant / pleasant
4. sharpener / sharp
5. fry / spy / by

Week 17: Activity 2

1. Mystery: what kind
2. I have a dentist appointment with Dr. Macdonald on Tues. Jan. 13.
3. Chuck's dog, Ringo, does not like his cat, Miss Kitty.
4. sailor is to ship as astronaut is to space shuttle
5. Hearts are to Valentine's Day as shamrocks are to St. Patrick's Day

Week 17: Activity 3

1. noun   2. verb
3. sore, soar   Answers will vary.
4. We have to fix the flat tire on our new car.
5. You did well on your geography project about Spain.

Week 17: Activity 4

1. opinion   2. fact
3. The Diamond Players Theatre is going to to a play called Sleeping Beauty.
4. "Have you ever heard the song called, 'Small World'?" asked the teacher.
5. predicate

Week 17: Activity 5

1. Donnie and I are going to the hockey game with dad.
2. They are selling tickets to the school play.
3. The monkeys climb up the walls of the cage every day.
4. Our team has 20 players and two coaches.
5. Bring a friend to the skating party on Saturday.

Bonus Activity: Analogies

1. Happy is to jolly as angry is to annoyed.
2. Claw is to cat as as pincer is to lobster.
3. Wet is to ocean as dry is to desert.
4. Walk is to run as whisper is to shout.
5. Milk is to carton as flower is to vase.
6. Beef is to cow as pork is to pig.
7. Brush is to painter as hammer is to carpenter.
8. Racquet is to tennis as club is to golf.

Week 18: Activity 1

1. synonyms
2. homophones
3. "I've got a big problem because I've lost my jacket," said Emma.
4. Please ask Aunt Lucy if she would like to come for dinner on Sunday.
5. verb

Week 18: Activity 2

1. Time went by quickly.
2. He couldn't sit still.
3. Has you ever been to the Calgary Stampede?
4. "I'm glad that Miss Harris is our gym teacher this year," said Penny.
5. Not a sentence

Week 18: Activity 3

1. The Rescue Canada helicopter flew right over our house on Friday.
2. We need to meet Tom at 8:00 or we'll be late.
3. suffix
4. prefix
5. Dear: salutation, greeting, opening

Week 18: Activity 4

1. page / painful / palace / panda / panic / parcel
2. The mechanic told us that our truck is going to be fixed on Tuesday.
3. If you don't wait for me, I won't be able to go with you.
4. At a hockey game
5. At a theatre performance

Week 18: Activity 5

1. atlas
2. encyclopedia
3. encyclopedia, atlas
4. thesaurus
5. dictionary

Bonus Activity: Sounds Like...

1. Horns / honk.   2. Raindrops / patter.   3. Coins / jingle.
4. Steam / hisses.   5. Whips / crack.   6. Fire / crackles.
7. Leaves / rustle.   8. Thunder / rumbles.   9. Bells / chime.

SSR1147   ISBN: 9781771587334 © On The Mark Press

WEEK 19: ACTIVITY 1

1. "Is it going to snow on Thursday or Friday?" asked Billy.
2. Have you ever gone skiing at Mont Tremblant, Quebec?
3. Fishing
4. easy – simple
5. cold / frosty, / freezing

WEEK 19: ACTIVITY 2

1. opposite
2. My coat is missing two buttons and it needs to be mended too.
3. I like sandwiches, cookies, milk, and an apple in my lunch.
4. Past
5. Future

WEEK 19: ACTIVITY 3

1. tuna / fruit / smooth
2. Predicate
3. Subject
4. Amelia, Carrie, and Molly went shopping with their cousin.
5. Do you have my number on your cellphone?

WEEK 19: ACTIVITY 4

1. doctor, nurse, paramedic, parent
2. weather forecaster
3. petrify
4. How old were you when you lost your first tooth?
5. Mom asked, "Did you finish all your homework last night?"

WEEK 19: ACTIVITY 5

1. Eats a lot; has a big appetite
2. They will be angry with me.
3. She is a very good swimmer.
4. She acts crazy; loses control.
5. Cause trouble; drive her crazy

BONUS ACTIVITY: LITTLE WORDS COUNT

1. Andy built the house by the creek.
2. Michael is good at football.
3. We put our trust in the doctor.
4. The dog jumped up on the little boy.
5. She does not agree with you.
6. We shall count on you to do well.
7. Sam is suffering from a bad cold.
8. Yesterday it was too hot to work.
9. The coats are hanging over there.
10. Dad gave Jim and me some candy.

WEEK 20: ACTIVITY 1

1. Earth is to planet as Sun is to star
2. handy: candy / handy /Mandy /Randy /Sandy
3. raid: laid /maid /paid /braid
4. The January Book Fair will be held at Lincoln Park Library.
5. My sister, Allison, is getting married on Sat. July 10, 2015.

WEEK 20: ACTIVITY 2

1. "Do you know the name of the boy who moved next door?" asked Grandma.
2. "Basketball practice is changed to Wednesday night," (our) coach reminded us.
3. fan – tas – tic
4. e – nor – mous
5. Toronto Blue Jays: baseball team

WEEK 20: ACTIVITY 3

1. Wednesday: Wed.   Thursday: Thurs.   Saturday: Sat.
2. His dog, Hector, has been trained to do four tricks.
3. Our doctor gave us our flu shot and it didn't hurt.
4. shouldn't: should not
5. they've: they have

WEEK 20: ACTIVITY 4

1. unreachable: reach
2. carelessly: care
3. Do you have any water, juice, or milk in your fridge that I could have?
4. He agreed to do his share and so their project got finished.
5. toaster / freezer / microwave / oven

WEEK 20: ACTIVITY 5

1. My black jacket has my name and the school crest on it.
2. We are having a birthday party for my grandmother when she turns 85 on Jan. 7.
3. The brown truck turned right and drove to the gas station.
4. I have younger twin brothers.
5. The truck that picks up our garbage comes on Thursday at 7 o'clock.

BONUS ACTIVITY: ACTION ! ACTION!

	sprint		whine
	rush		spy
	fast	scatter	
	bounce		smile
twist		growl	

WEEK 21: ACTIVITY 1

1. Tiny fish
2. Serious and difficult
3. Eddie went to to Regina, Saskatchewan to watch the Roughriders play football.
4. He and she have the same jacket on today, don't they?
5. removed: move

WEEK 21: ACTIVITY 2

1. Mom gave us a choice between hot dogs or french fries for lunch.
2. The movie called The Littlest Elf is a Christmas favourite of mine.
3. learn / burn / fern / turn / tern
4. him / dim / trim / limb
5. homophones

WEEK 21: ACTIVITY 3

1. Place your items on the counter so the cashier can scan them. Supermarket, department store
2. Alice and I made up a song for our play called In the Dark Forest.
3. Our school, Sir Winston Churchill, is the greatest school in Nova Scotia.
4. Fact
5. Fantasy

WEEK 21: ACTIVITY 4

1. In Grade Two, I brought my pet hamster, Ollie, to school for Show and Tell.
2. "Will you pour me a glass of icy cold milk?" asked Teddy
3. unlucky: luck
4. misunderstanding: understand
5. same: different

WEEK 21: ACTIVITY 5

1. dictionary
2. atlas
3. encyclopedia
4. almanac
5. thesaurus

BONUS ACTIVITY: CHAIN WORDS

1. an   2. pan   3. soon   4. bacon   5. so   6. sea
7. sale

WEEK 22: ACTIVITY 1

1. Opinion
2. Fact
3. nasty
4. Shawn is going to visit his grandfather next weekend in Kelowna, British Columbia.
5. We broke Mom's lamp and now she will be angry at us.

WEEK 22: ACTIVITY 2

1. unreliable: 5
2. They
3. her
4. Our flight to from Toronto International Airport to Dawson City left at 8:00.
5. The primary colours are red, blue, and yellow. They can be mixed to make new colours.

WEEK 22: ACTIVITY 3

1. everywhere / telescope / hopefully
2. opening / direction / understand
3. fruit
4. Chris brought his comic book collection to show our class.
5. My sister doesn't want to help me do my math homework.

SSR1147   ISBN: 9781771587334 © On The Mark Press

Week 22: Activity 4

1. Firefighter
2. "Let's plan a surprise birthday party for Dad," Mom whispered.
3. My uncle Henry works at Canada's weather station in the Arctic.
4. Make it up; lie about it
5. His job or career

Week 22: Activity 5

1. My cousin doesn't have any serious allergies.
2. We celebrate Valentine's Day on February 14.
3. The basketball player tossed the ball through the hoop and scored.
4. Miss Graves gave us a second chance to learn our spelling words.
5. Celia and I take dance lessons on Tuesdays after school.

Bonus Activity: Riddle Me This!

1. clock   2. river   3. chair   4. jug   5. saw   6. fence
7. needle   8. kite

Week 23: Activity 1

1. Who won the basketball game when you played the Raiders?
2. Did you feel any pressure to score points for your team?
3. Hard to understand; mixed up
4. hang
5. stony

Week 23: Activity 2

1. We swam all day at the beach. We went to sleep early.
2. Abby and Sarah are learning to dive because they want to be on the swim team.
3. Past
4. Future
5. should not: shouldn't

Week 23: Activity 3

1. Mr. Thoms taught us how to make awesome sand castles.
2. "I didn't expect to see you out here so late," said my Uncle Howard.
3. synonyms
4. at – ten – tion
5. grand – fa – ther

Week 23: Activity 4

1. Your friend, Harry – closing / signature
2. good: hood / wood / could / should / would
3. gave: brave / shave / wave / crave / pave
4. Jake and Larry are good friends. They are in the same grade too.
5. Janet and I are going shopping at the West Edmonton Mall on Friday.

Week 23: Activity 5

1. No mistake
2. Punctuation error
3. Punctuation error
4. Capitalization error
5. Spelling error

Bonus Activity: Whether the Weather...

1. foggy   2. stormy   3. rainy   4. humid   5. frosty
6. cloudy   7. mild   8. breezy

Week 24: Activity 1

1. A person who draws maps and charts
2. Mr. Howard said, "Tonight's homework is to review the chapter on Jacques Cartier".
3. Do you have any puppies for sale?
4. bird is to sky as fish is to water.
5. lettuce is to green as tomato is to red.

Week 24: Activity 2

1. hop: hops / hopped / hopping
2. come: comes / coming
3. Do you know what you are doing for your science project?
4. Ralph is learning how to play golf with his Uncle Fred.
5. Exclamatory

Week 24: Activity 3

1. My friends and I
2. Our class went on a field trip to Casa Loma in Toronto on Tues. May 23, 2015.
3. Everyone loved the ride called The Big Zipper at the local fair.
4. It   5. she

WEEK 24: ACTIVITY 4

1. She and I wanted to prove that we didn't break Mom's favourite dish.
2. The diver swam near the wreck to sea if there was a treasure inside.
3. give / gave
4. run / ran
5. What time does the adventure movie start? – verb

WEEK 24: ACTIVITY 5

1. Fighting with each other.
2. She had a big smile.
3. He was very fast.
4. They are very stubborn.
5. Not able to concentrate or focus

BONUS ACTIVITY: ADVERBS! ADVERBS!

quickly		roughly	
	sleepily		
	lazily		brightly
loudly	proudly	angrily	
noisily			dimly

WEEK 25: ACTIVITY 1

1. We are trying to memorize the poem, "Indian Summer".
2. "Which mall has a movie theatre showing Into the Deep?" asked Jane.
3. the shoes of the shoemaker: the shoemaker's shoes
4. the pool of the hotel: the hotel's pool
5. She'd: she had

WEEK 25: ACTIVITY 2

1. My favourite NHL teams are the Edmonton Oilers and the Calgary Flames.
2. My brother Andy likes the Ottawa Senators and the Vancouver Canucks.
3. newt
4. Nunavut: 3
5. Nova Scotia: 4

WEEK 25: ACTIVITY 3

1. simile
2. metaphor
3. Our parents announced to the family, "We are going to visit the Yukon in July."
4. Dad read the story The Littlest Bear to me and Amy at bedtime.
5. 1–elbow   3–elk   5–email   4–elm   2–elephant

WEEK 25: ACTIVITY 4

1. Dad shouted, "Bring me the rope hanging on the wall in the shed."
2. On Saturday, Michael gave me the book called The Lost Boy to read.
3. There are a few cookies left in the cookie jar. How many
4. Fantasy
5. Fact

WEEK 25: ACTIVITY 5

1. atlas
2. encyclopedia
3. dictionary
4. almanac, encyclopedia
5. thesaurus

BONUS ACTIVITY: DICTIONARY DETECTIVE

1. b   2. a   3. c   4. b   5. b   6. b   7. c   8. a   9. c   10. c

WEEK 26: ACTIVITY 1

1. Future
2. Past
3. Betsy said, "I'm bringing sandwiches, cookies, and juice boxes to the picnic."
4. When I went to the circus on Saturday, I saw a man high up on a trapeze.
5. Sept.

WEEK 26: ACTIVITY 2

1. Brazil is to South America as Canada is to North America
2. apple is to tree as berry is to bush
3. dis – ap – pear
4. Uncle Bob visited us on his way to Regina, Saskatchewan.
5. In June I am going to be in my cousin Ashley's wedding.

SSR1147   ISBN: 9781771587334 © On The Mark Press

Week 26: Activity 3

1. subject   2. object
3. "Boys and girls, listen for a minute, please", said our soccer coach.
4. "How far is it to Kingston from here?" asked the tourist.
5. cry / cried / will cry

Week 26: Activity 4

1. Alice went to the dentist on Monday and was given a new red toothbrush.
2. Mr. Jones was working on his lawnmower and finally fixed it.
3. adjective   4. verb
5. bear, bare   Answers will vary.

Week 26: Activity 5

1. The students debated the topic of school uniforms but they did not reach a conclusion.
2. Mom was surprised when she got yellow daffodils for Mother's Day.
3. Dad and I went to Pizza Palace on James Street and had the Super Special.
4. My delicious sundae was made with chocolate ice cream, chocolate syrup and sprinkles.
5. I have an awesome pet iguana named Hector.

Bonus Activity: Name That Place!

1. Planks are made from logs at a sawmill.
2. Stone is dug from a quarry.
3. Cars are made in a factory.
4. Bread is baked at a bakery.
5. Plants are grown and sold at a nursery.
6. Clothes are washed at a laundromat.
7. Books are stored and loaned from a library.

Week 27: Activity 1

1. Our school vacation begins on June 24, 2014 and ends on September 4, 2014.
2. Grandpa bought hot dogs and french fries for us to eat on the Annual Scouts Picnic.
3. haven't: have not
4. would've: would have
5. the colour of the pony: the pony's colour

Week 27: Activity 2

1. draggon
2. culamity
3. uniforms: 3
4. They are moving to a new house at 1427 Apple Hill Lane.
5. The leaves blew off the trees and into our yard.

Week 27: Activity 3

1. Items used to make something look better or beautiful.
2. concentrate
3. "Does you want to go to see the movie Lost Land with me?" asked Jared.
4. Willy's dog, Buddy, chased my cat, Fuzzy, down Maple Street on Sunday.
5. Future

Week 27: Activity 4

1. today / paint / they
2. Dean blew out all twelve candles on his birthday cake.
3. My ice cream sundae was covered with syrup, berries, and peanuts.
4. read
5. rang

Week 27: Activity 5

1. Brandon and I are invited to the birthday party.
2. The boys had a good time at the basketball game.
3. Chris drove the car really well for a beginner.
4. Will you pass me the potatoes, please?
5. If we play well, we will win the championship game.

Bonus Activity: When I hear "Canada", I think of...

```
                          L
H                    M  O  O  S  E
O     C              A     O           R
C  N     R  C  M  P  N              O
K  T              L     I           C
E  P  O  U  T  I  N  E     E        K
Y  W              L  L                 I
   E        T  O  T  E  M  P  O  L  E  S
   R           B  E  A  V  E  R        S
                    F
P  O  L  A  R  B  E  A  R
```

WEEK 28: ACTIVITY 1

1. That is a <u>beautiful</u> bouquet of flowers. adjective
2. Her skating dress <u>sparkles</u> when she jumps. verb
3. Have you ever sang the song "God Save the Queen"?
4. Canada's queen is Queen Elizabeth II who lives in England.
5. digs

WEEK 28: ACTIVITY 2

1. On a hill for sledding or tobogganing.
2. Jackson's baseball team has two outs and two strikes.
3. We are going to have a visit from Sparky the Fire Safety Dog tomorrow.
4. Fiction
5. Fact

WEEK 28: ACTIVITY 3

1. body
2. closing
3. Fast food restaurant
4. He rides a mountain bike that has red flames.
5. The baby robin waited for its mother to bring it a worm.

WEEK 28: ACTIVITY 4

1. multiplication is to division as addition is to subtraction.
2. We're saving money by using our coupons to buy food and other things.
3. She doesn't like the taste of chocolate but she does like strawberry.
4. On a street / sidewalk
5. In the kitchen

WEEK 28: ACTIVITY 5

1. Capitalization error
2. No error.
3. Punctuation error
4. Spelling error
5. Punctuation error

BONUS ACTIVITY: BUZZ! FLUTTER! FLY!

1. A <u>mosquito</u> sucks blood.
2. The <u>bee</u> makes honey.
3. A <u>cricket</u> sings in the summer.
4. A <u>firefly</u> glows in the dark of night.
5. A <u>ladybug</u> has spots on its back.
6. A <u>moth</u> flies at night.
7. The <u>butterfly</u> is brightly coloured.
8. If a <u>wasp</u> stings you, it will hurt.

WEEK 29: ACTIVITY 1

1. Our class made a graph to show information about favourite places to visit in Canada.
2. Mom's car broke down on her way home so she called a tow truck.
3. teeth: plural
4. toothbrush: singular
5. I'm: I am

WEEK 29: ACTIVITY 2

1. He and she have the lead parts in the play <u>Anne of Green Gables</u>.
2. Jeff, the weather man, gave us the long range forecast for Victoria, British Columbia.
3. Smell, odour
4. very excited, happy
5. Interrogative

WEEK 29: ACTIVITY 3

1. In Banff, Alberta we got to go skiing with our Uncle George.
2. "We will feed the sheep after we groom the horse," said Tom.
3. Nahanni National Park: proper
4. campfire: common
5. Who is the girl wearing the red and black dress?
   – red, black

WEEK 29: ACTIVITY 4

1. confusion: confuse
2. swimming: swim
3. The spectators clapped loudly when he scored the winning goal.
4. Miss Vogel said, "We will have the final test in history on Thursday, January 30.
5. va – ca – tion

WEEK 29: ACTIVITY 5

1. Did you sense people were talking about you?
2. In trouble
3. Saying great things about you.
4. Good luck!
5. It is raining really hard.

SSR1147   ISBN: 9781771587334 © On The Mark Press

Bonus Activity: Animal Unscramble

1. wolf
2. polar bear
3. red fox
4. caribou
5. lynx
6. grizzly bear
7. chipmunk
8. buffalo

Week 30: Activity 1

1. he'll: he will
2. Ava is going to borrow Grace's blue dress for the party on Saturday.
3. Evan, Ted, and Grant went with their dad to buy new bikes.
4. breakfast
5. elbow

Week 30: Activity 2

1. Opinion
2. Miss Leader, Mrs. Martin, and Mr. Cummings all teach at Hartford Elementary School.
3. Sarah and Louis took pictures of animals at Granby Zoo.
4. situation: 4
5. demolition: 4

Week 30: Activity 3

1. I just finished reading a book called Emily of New Moon by L. M. Montgomery.
2. "May I borrow your ruler and eraser?" Alex whispered.
3. yesterday is to past as tomorrow is to future
4. 4–clover   3–cleaver   2–clean   1–clam   5–clump
5. 2–marsh   4–mind   3–mention   1–many   5–mood

Week 30: Activity 4

1. "I don't have any time to waste. I'm late!" shouted Quentin.
2. "I've picked up a nail in my new tire!" exclaimed Mrs. Foster.
3. past
4. Adverb
5. verb

Week 30: Activity 5

1. atlas
2. dictionary
3. encyclopedia, almanac
4. thesaurus
5. dictionary

Bonus Activity: Yum! Poutine!

One Syllable: cheese, curds, bowl, fries
Two Syllables: gravy, gooey, tasty, messy
Four Syllables: Canadian

Week 31: Activity 1

1. necessary
2. beginning
3. Fred fell on the ice and he broke his right wrist.
4. In February we have Spirit Week at Blackburn Middle School.
5. cry: cried

Week 31: Activity 2

1. Opinion   2. Fact
3. "How many books did you read this summer?" asked the librarian.
4. Do you want to go tobogganing with us on Big Ben Hill?
5. The traffic light turned green, (so we walked across the street).

Week 31: Activity 3

1. wealthy, poor   Answers will vary.
2. hardworking, lazy   Answers will vary.
3. Gus will meet us at the movies. – future
4. He called Max, his best friend, to find out the time of the game.
5. "Will you deliver this package for me?" Mr. Woods asked.

Week 31: Activity 4

1. What kind
2. Jen and Beth needed an hour to get ready for the party.
3. Your grandparents live too far away to visit very often, don't they?
4. Opinion   5. Fact

WEEK 31: ACTIVITY 5

1. The score in the game was a very close 5 to 4 but we won!
2. That test was easy because I studied for two hours last night.
3. We visited the new science museum that shows the history of technology.
4. It rained so hard all day that the streets were flooded and some cars got stuck.
5. Penny dove into the pool, held her breath and swam underwater.

BONUS ACTIVITY: FOLLOW THAT ADJECTIVE!

START — deep — red — pretty — cold — green — heavy — sunny — strong — small — powerful — huge — FINISH

WEEK 32: ACTIVITY 1

1. Tim and Peggy are getting married and moving to Cornerbrook, Newfoundland.
2. "How many times do you want me to tell you this story?" Mom asked.
3. space
4. neat   5. late

WEEK 32: ACTIVITY 2

1. In an elevator
2. The blizzard began at 7:30 a.m. and ended at 2:30 p.m.
3. Before you begin to cook, gather all your ingredients and utensils.
4. Opinion   5. Fact

WEEK 32: ACTIVITY 3

1. messy / messier / messiest
2. good / better / best
3. Grandma's group of friends meet at Tim Horton's every Tuesday morning.
4. He and I got paid for shovelling snow at Mrs. Fletcher's house.
5. lit – ter – bug

WEEK 32: ACTIVITY 4

1. The baby laughed when the toy squeaked.
2. Dr. Franklin is a good dentist because she is very careful.
3. They will name their baby Bella if it is a girl and Patrick if it is a boy.
4. strawberry is to red as banana is to yellow
5. evening is to dinner as morning is to breakfast

WEEK 32: ACTIVITY 5

1. Which side did you take in the debate?
2. Can we wade to the middle of the pond?
3. If we are going to sell cookies, we want to make a profit.
4. Rosa wore a bright red ribbon in her hair to match her dress.
5. Tyler's black lab had eight puppies on Sunday.

BONUS ACTIVITY: A NOT–SO–SECRET MESSAGE!

Canada is great!

SSR1147   ISBN: 9781771587334 © On The Mark Press